ISBN 978-0-266-78062-5
PIBN 10968064

1 MONTH OF
FREE
READING

at

www.ForgottenBooks.com

By purchasing this book you are eligible for one month membership to ForgottenBooks.com, giving you unlimited access to our entire collection of over 1,000,000 titles via our web site and mobile apps.

To claim your free month visit: www.forgottenbooks.com/free968064

English
Français
Deutsche
Italiano
Español
Português

www.forgottenbooks.com

Mythology Photography **Fiction**
Fishing Christianity **Art** Cooking
Essays Buddhism Freemasonry
Medicine **Biology** Music **Ancient**
Egypt Evolution Carpentry Physics
Dance Geology **Mathematics** Fitness
Shakespeare **Folklore** Yoga Marketing
Confidence Immortality Biographies
Poetry **Psychology** Witchcraft
Electronics Chemistry History **Law**
Accounting **Philosophy** Anthropology
Alchemy Drama Quantum Mechanics
Atheism Sexual Health **Ancient History**
Entrepreneurship Languages Sport
Paleontology Needlework Islam
Metaphysics Investment Archaeology
Parenting Statistics Criminology
Motivational

FORES
WORKER

January, 1931

Issued bimonthly by the FOREST SERVICE
UNITED STATES DEPARTMENT OF AGRICULTURE

CONTENTS

	Page
State forestry	1
Education and extension	5
Forest Service notes	8
General forest news	14
Foreign notes	19
Personals	22
Bibliography	24

Announcements

Western Forestry and Conservation Association Meeting

The annual meeting and Pacific Coast forest conference of the Western Forestry and Conservation Association will be held in Spokane, Wash., March 19-21, with headquarters in the Davenport Hotel. As usual, the first day will be devoted to affairs of the protection and educational committees. On the second and third days, phases of forest growing and protection will be discussed.

Second Spanish National Congress of Lumber and Lumber Industries

Spain's second National Congress of Lumber and Lumber Industries will be held in Madrid in May, 1931. It will continue the work initiated at the first congress, held in Barcelona in 1929. The organizing committee of the congress includes representatives of the national institute of forest research and many national associations such as those of wood importers, cork producers, and paper manufacturers.

The FOREST WORKER is published by the Forest Service, United States Department of Agriculture, Washington, D. C. Jean Kerr, editor. Material offered for publication in the FOREST WORKER should be addressed to the editor.

Because the free edition is necessarily limited, this periodical can be distributed without charge outside of the Government service only to such persons and organizations as State forestry and conservation officials, State agricultural extension directors, faculties and libraries of forest schools, and forestry associations. Others desiring to obtain copies of the FOREST WORKER can do so by sending 5 cents for a single copy or 25 cents for a year's subscription to the Superintendent of Documents, Government Printing Office, Washington, D. C. Foreign subscriptions: Yearly, 35 cents; single copies, 7 cents.

OREST WORKER

Washington, D. C.   JANUARY, 1931   Vol. 7, No. 1

State Forestry

New York Acquires 40,000 Acres for Reforestation under Hewitt Act

Within the year 1930 the New York Conservation Department acquired more than 40,000 acres of land for development as production forests, under provisions of the Hewitt law of 1929. The cost averaged $3.70 per acre. The land acquired consists of 48 areas, ranging from 500 acres to more than 3,600 acres, in 14 counties. All the areas to which title has been approved have been planted, the planting requiring more than 7,000,000 trees. Planting costs per 1,000 trees ranged from $2.05 for trees planted with the use of a machine to $7.31 for trees planted by hand. All the new plantations have been protected against forest fires with fire lines consisting of six furrows each. The 45.27 miles of fire line required cost $22.05 per mile. To protect the plantations of northern white pine from the blister rust, currant and gooseberry bushes were removed from 2,430 acres of land in the vicinity of such plantations at a cost of about 50 cents per acre.

In the year ending September 30, 1930, New York enlarged its State forest preserve by 40,142 acres, including 22,242 acres in the Adirondacks and 17,900 acres in the Catskills. These lands cost on the average $9.33 per acre. The outstanding purchase of the year in the Catskills is a tract of more than 2,000 acres including the so-called Westkill or Deer Notch.

Fires Few along Cleared Roadsides in California

In 23 out of 28 California counties reporting, not a single fire occurred in 1930 along roadsides which the State division of highways had cleared, State Forester Pratt announces. In the five remaining counties only seven fires along such roadsides were reported. Along highways that had not been cleared, 89 fires occurred in the 28 counties during the year. Under the State's new roadside clearing program, highway crews on construction or maintenance work clear away the weeds, brush, and other débris along roadsides by spraying them with oil and burning them. Before the burning is done the State obtains the consent of owners of roadside property.

Proposed State Forest for California

By J. H. PRICE, United States Forest Service

An exchange of forest land between the Federal Government and the State of California was recently completed through which the State obtains a consolidated block of 8,973 acres along the western boundary of the Lassen National Forest, in Shasta County. The State gives in exchange a somewhat greater area consisting of scattered school sections within the national forest boundaries.

Since school lands were used to acquire the Shasta County area, the area can not yet be considered strictly a State forest. It is proposed to introduce legislation to pay into the State school funds the amount of the appraised value of the school lands involved in the exchange, and thus make it possible to establish a State forest in the strictest sense of the term. If such legislation is approved the State will have a forest property of a permanent character and one that can be largely extended to the north, west, and south, since the adjacent lands in these directions are all privately owned.

The Shasta County area has been carefully mapped and cruised. It is estimated that there is 100,000,000 feet of merchantable timber on the area. Most of this timber is concentrated on a small portion of the block, thus constituting a perfectly merchantable stand. The remainder of the block is made up chiefly of reproducing brush lands. These brush fields are the result of fires that occurred prior to the period of protection, many of the fires probably antedating the coming of white men to the country. The young growth is coming in very fast on account of the protection given the area during the past 20 years, and much of it is now reaching pole size. With continued protection, the forest should regenerate itself over the entire area without planting.

The merchantable stand consists in a mixture of western yellow pine, sugar pine, incense cedar, and

1

white fir. The young growth that is replacing the brush consists of these same species; but the greater portion of it is white fir, since the brush fields are located principally on areas that most readily produce this species.

New York Equipped to Extract Seed from 10,000 Bushels of Cones a Year

More than 2 tons of tree seed will be used in 1931 in New York State's forest nurseries. When a new unit recently purchased at Willsboro has been added to its seed-extracting plants, however, the State conservation department will be able to fill its own seed requirements almost entirely in years when the cone crop is good. Extraction plants at the State's Lake Clear and Saratoga forest nurseries have a capacity of about 3,000 bushels of cones each, and the one at Willsboro has a capacity of about 4,000 bushels. Operation of the plants at Willsboro, Lake Clear, and Saratoga will cut in half the State's annual seed bill. For 1931 this will be about $12,000.

The Willsboro plant is located in the heart of the northern white pine and Norway pine region.

In years of good cone crops the department can obtain within the boundaries of New York as many cones as it needs of northern white pine, Norway pine, white spruce, northern white cedar, and balsam fir. Thus far it has had to import from Europe its supplies of seed of black locust, European larch, and Norway spruce. In 1930 the local Norway pine cone crop failed completely and the department found it necessary to buy 4,500 bushels of Norway pine cones in Minnesota.

The State's present planting program calls for production of approximately 75,000,000 3-year-old trees in 1934. To fulfill this program 11,000 seed beds must be planted with from 4 to .12 ounces of seed each, according to species.

❦

Educational work is now a full-time job for one man in the Virginia Forest Service. James P. Andrews, formerly district forester for the Piedmont section of the State, has been transferred to this work. At present Mr. Andrews is traveling through the State in a truck equipped for showing motion pictures and stereopticon views.

❦

The Georgia Forest Service has begun publication, with a January, 1931, number, of the Georgia Forest Lookout, a 4-page monthly news-letter. The Lookout is to be an organ not only of the Georgia Forest Service but of the Georgia Forestry Association, the 32 timber-protective organizations in Georgia, and the State's vocational schools. The editor is C. A. Whittle, director of education of the Georgia Forest Service.

Central States Forestry Congress Organized

The Central States Forestry Congress held its first meeting in Indianapolis December 3–5, 1930. Each of the seven States of Illinois, Indiana, Iowa, Kentucky, Missouri, Ohio, and Tennessee took an active part in organizing the congress. Michigan, West Virginia, and Wisconsin, also, had representatives at the Indianapolis meeting. The State foresters of all the actively participating States served on the arrangements committee, together with E. F. McCarthy, director of the Central States Forest Experiment Station, and some 25 private citizens. E. Murray Bruner, Federal forest inspector in the Central States, was chairman of the committee. The Indiana Department of Conservation financed the meeting.

In this first meeting it was thought better to discuss many different features of the forestry situation in the Central States than to concentrate on one or a very few of its aspects. Possibly the greatest emphasis was given to farm forestry and forest research. The character of the program is reflected in the series of resolutions adopted by the congress. These urge that the agricultural colleges of the region, on the basis of a policy of complete land use in their respective States, include training in farm woodland management as a requirement in all regular agricultural courses; call to the attention of members of the Federal Congress and of heads of Federal administrative departments the need for erosion-control research and request that adequate funds be provided for studying this problem and developing control methods through forestry practices; urge upon all the States in the central group the establishment of forest nurseries adequate to produce forest planting stock in quantities to meet their respective needs; urge legislation to provide adequate protection for forest land within participating States; recommend to the Federal Government the provision of additional funds for accelerating the work of the forest survey of the United States now being carried on under the terms of the McSweeney-McNary law, and to the State Governments provision for an early beginning in collecting data on forest and idle land; commend the program of the national forest reservation commission, and urge that increased funds be speedily provided to permit more rapid expansion of this program.

Although the meeting was largely in the hands of professional foresters the program included such speakers as Richard Lieber, director of the Indiana Department of Conservation; Edward C. Elliott, president of Purdue University; Frank S. Betz, retired manufacturer of Hammond, Ind.; W. E. Tharpe, soil specialist of the United States Department of Agriculture; G. ☙. Young, farm management specialist of Purdue University; R. W. Brown, president of the Missouri Farm Bureau; John I. Shafer, president of the National

Hardwood Lumbermen's Association; and R. J. Plaster, agricultural agent of the New York Central Lines.

Official registration at the meeting totaled 132.

Permanent organization of the congress was effected through adoption of a constitution, and a board of 15 directors was elected.

The third day of the meeting was given over to an automobile trip to the newly purchased Morgan-Monroe Counties State Forest of Indiana, situated some 35 miles southwest of Indianapolis.

It is planned to hold the 1931 meeting of the congress in Cincinnati, Ohio.

Indiana State Nursery Prepares for Large Plantings

Between 800 and 900 bushels of black walnuts have been stratified at the Clark County State forest nursery of Indiana in preparation for planting in the spring of 1931. Woodland owners, county agents, and school teachers cooperated in collecting the walnuts and shipping them to the nursery. Approximately 700,000 Norway spruce, northern white pine, and Norway pine seedlings have been transplanted at the nursery in preparation for planting in 1933.

The Clark County forest nursery has a new reservoir with five times the capacity of the old one.

A New State Park for Michigan

Land valued at $65,000 in the Irish Hills of Michigan has been given to the State by Mercy J. Hayes, of Detroit, for development as a State park, in memory of her brother, the late Senator Walter J. Hayes. The property has an area of 466 acres, includes the whole 60-acre expanse of Round Lake and more than one-half mile frontage on Wamplers Lake, fronts on United States Route 112, and is within 60 miles of Detroit, Toledo, Jackson, Battle Creek, and Lansing. The new park will incorporate the Cedar Hills Park, organized some time ago as the only State park in southeastern Michigan.

Michigan now has 66 State park sites, containing 29,146 acres and having an appraised valuation of $2,123,150. Lands given to the State represent a large part of this valuation, and some of the other lands were acquired through tax delinquency. The State's expenditure in acquiring park sites, in fact, totals less than $250,000. The Michigan State park system was begun 11 years ago. By July 1, 1931, the State will have spent approximately $1,250,000 on developing and maintaining State parks.

❦

Five minutes each Friday noon are allotted to the Mississippi Forest Service by WJDX, the Lamar Life Insurance Co. broadcasting station in Jackson, Miss., under the head of State's Business.

Florida to Give $9,000 Worth of Firebreak Demonstrations this Year

To encourage Florida timberland owners to construct firebreaks, many thousand miles of which are needed for the protection of longleaf and slash pine stands in the State, the Florida Forest Service is conducting a demonstration project on which it expects to spend $9,000 within the current fiscal year. The project is to some degree experimental; its results are expected to help determine what kind of firebreak and what type of firebreak equipment are best for the Florida pine forests. A McCormick-Deering "Farmall" tractor and a Taylor double-disk plow are being used. The tractor is transported on a 1½-ton Ford truck; the plow and small equipment are carried on a trailer. The demonstrator is assisted by a mechanic who drives the truck and the tractor. Other makes and types of plows will be tried out.

One of the most satisfactory types of firebreak thus far constructed consists in a 7-foot plowed strip made with one trip of the double-disk plow, the soil being thrown each way from the center. This makes a fairly clean break except for a 6 to 10 inch unplowed ridge in the center. An effort is being made to design a third disk to turn over this center strip.

Demonstrations are carried out on land the owners or lessees of which agree to furnish the gasoline and oil for the tractor and the labor needed to clear logs from the right of way. The demonstrator constructs the necessary firebreaks on one-fifth of the part of the property that needs firebreaks, or on at least two sections of land. In arranging for demonstrations preference is given first to turpentine orchards on protection units, next to other land on protection units, and next to turpentine orchards adjacent to or in the vicinity of protection units.

❦

California had a forestry force of 178 in the field in 1930. In addition the State employed from 6 to 8 men in the forest nursery at Davis, where planting stock is grown for the use of State institutions and for distribution to farmers. The State's 1930 expenditures for forestry purposes were estimated at $325,000. County funds available during the year for forestry activities supervised by the State amounted to $140,000.

❦

A museum of Louisiana's natural resources and a lecture hall equipped for showing films and slides have been established by the Louisiana Department of Conservation on Royal Street, New Orleans, 1½ blocks from Canal Street. The museum is open to the public without charge, from 10 a. m. to 6 p. m. daily; motion pictures are screened daily and by appointment.

Delaware's First Steps in State Forestry

The beginnings of State forestry in Delaware are recounted by State Forester William S. Taber in a printed report for the period July 1, 1929–June 30, 1930, including a summary of activities in the two preceding years. It was in August of 1927 that the Delaware Forestry Commission came into existence, under provisions of a law enacted in that year.

According to United States census figures, the area of land used for farm crop production in the 1,257,600-acre State of Delaware decreased by more than 40,000 acres in the period 1920-1930. Natural regeneration of pine is expected to reclaim much of the abandoned land in the southern part of the State. In order to grow trees for planting on other abandoned lands, in the spring of 1928 the State forestry commission provided itself with a 4-acre nursery site by purchase and lease of land along the Du Pont Road adjacent to Hudson Pond. The 1929 inventory showed that the nursery contained 648,000 seedlings. While awaiting the opportunity to distribute trees of its own growing the forestry department has purchased 197,950 trees and sold them to Delaware landowners at a nominal charge for forest planting.

A 46-acre tract situated along the Du Pont Road near Ellendale has been purchased as a State forest. Thinning and pruning operations have been carried out on portions of this area, and on portions not fully stocked with trees demonstration and experimental plantings have been made with loblolly pine, cypress, and Asiatic chestnuts. An area of 5 acres along Red Lion Creek, New Castle County, presented by General and Mrs. Coleman Du Pont will be planted with trees this spring in preparation for being opened eventually as a State forest park.

A forest survey has thus far covered 47,057 acres of land in Sussex County. Mr. Taber estimates that approximately 380,000 acres of land in Delaware is stocked with either timber or brush. Of this area 350,000 acres, he estimates, supports a forest growth capable under correct management of producing at least one-half cord of wood per acre per year.

Much of the effort of Mr. Taber and his assistant, Carl P. Fatzinger, is devoted to public education through illustrated lectures, newspaper articles, and publications.

Recently the State forestry department prepared plans to be used by the State highway commission in establishing ornamental plantings along the dual highway between State Road and St. George's.

Under provisions of the Clarke-McNary law Delaware is receiving allotments of Federal funds for use in distributing planting stock and preventing forest fires. For forest fire detection and suppression the State legislature has not as yet appropriated any funds. The State highway police report fires to the forestry department, and the volunteer fire companies in the State have without exception given service in suppressing forest fires. The forestry department instructs the volunteer suppression forces in fire-control methods, supplies them with fire-fighting apparatus, and supervises their efforts on the fire line. In 1930, volunteer fire wardens reported 143 fires covering 28,546 acres between January 1 and October 15.

New York Camp Grounds Have 267,886 Registration in 1930

Campers registered at New York State's large public camp sites numbered 267,886 in 1930, which is twice the 1929 registration and seven times that of 1927. This figure does not include picnickers and others who used the grounds less than a day, or campers at public grounds other than the large camp grounds having resident rangers in charge. In the past three years the State's camp grounds of the latter description have increased in number from 9 to 17 and several of them have been more than doubled in size.

New York's public recreation grounds other than those for which registration is quoted include island property in Lake George, 11 recreational developments on the St. Lawrence reservation, and more than 100 small public camp sites in the Adirondacks and Catskills.

A recent purchase brought into State ownership 4,040 acres of land in the Paradox tract, in Essex County, containing some highly desirable sites for public camps. The land consists for the most part of scattered lots adjoining land owned by the State or under contract. It includes frontage on Johnson Pond, Paradox Lake, and Eagle Lake, and is crossed by the Schroon Lake-Ticonderoga State highway and also the so-called Johnson Pond Road.

For this land the State paid $21,603, or approximately $5.30 per acre.

❧

Through action of North Carolina and Tennessee conservation authorities 12,000 acres of the French Broad division of the Pisgah National Forest has become the Andrew Johnson Interstate Game Refuge. Approximately half the refuge area lies on each side of the State line. The two States will share administration costs on an equal basis, but the Tennessee game officials have agreed to leave the direction of the refuge altogether in the hands of the North Carolina game warden service.

❧

A calendar issued by the Florida Forest Service for 1931 pictures a scene in a turpentining operation and bears the slogan "Liquid Gold from Thrifty Pines: Keep it Flowing." Legends in smaller lettering state essentials of good turpentining practice.

Twenty counties of New York State carried out forestry projects in 1930 under the Hewitt law of 1929 which authorizes the State to match county appropriations for reforestation purposes up to $5,000 per county per year. The counties invested $67,556, the State $48,832.

❦

Since August 15, 1930, there have been added to Maryland's State forest possessions a tract of 1,200 acres near Doncaster, in Charles County, and one of 2,600 acres in the vicinity of Cedarville, partly in Charles and partly in Prince Georges County. These additions brought the total area of Maryland State forests to 25,000 acres.

❦

A 100-foot steel observation tower with inside stairway has been completed by the North Carolina Forest Service a mile east of Chadbourn, in Columbus County, on North Carolina Highway No. 20. The site was given to the State by C. R. Bailey, of Chadbourn. This is the twenty-second tower in the State's fire-detection system.

On June 30, 1930, Michigan held title to 603,475 acres of State forest lands, an increase of 231,171 acres over the total so held at the end of the fiscal year 1927-28. Of the acreage added during the biennium tax delinquency accounted for 176,600; purchase, for 38,536; exchange, for 15,398; and gift, for 637.

❦

Alabama's first State park was recently established by Governor Graves under authority of an act of September 6, 1927. The park is located on the banks of the Coosa River, in the southwestern part of Talladega County, about a mile east of Owen's Ferry, and has an area of 421 acres.

❦

A steel observation tower has been erected on the Warm Springs, Ga., timber protective organization area by Georgia Wilkins, Columbus, Ga., as a memorial to her uncle, Charles Davis, for many years owner of the Warm Springs property. The tower was dedicated on December 8 by Gov. Franklin D. Roosevelt.

Education and Extension

Idaho University Institutes Wood Chemistry Research

Work in the chemical utilization of wood and studies in forest chemistry have been instituted in the forest products laboratories of the University of Idaho, of which E. E. Hubert has charge. Research in forest chemistry is being conducted by E. C. Jahn, a wood and cellulose chemist who received training under L. H. Wise, of the New York State College of Forestry, and Harold Hibbert, of the Pulp and Paper Institute of McGill University, and who studied the pulp and paper industry in Sweden during the past year as a fellow of the American-Scandinavian Foundation.

New Haven Property Given to Yale for Botanical and Forestry Use

Property at the corner of Edwards and Prospect Streets, New Haven, Conn., which was the home of the late William Whitman Farnum, former treasurer of Yale University, has been given to the university to be used by the schools of forestry and botany as the William Whitman Farnum Memorial Garden. The gift includes a maintenance fund. The donor is Mrs. Vincent Ardenghi, widow of Mr. Farnum. Mrs. Ardenghi has suggested that the house included in the property might be used as a home for the president of the university, but has stated that if the Yale Corporation decides to tear down the house in order to erect a building for the use of the school of botany or the school of forestry the plan will be acceptable to her. The greenhouse is to be put to use immediately in connection with botanical work of the university, and it is planned to administer the grounds as a supplement to the Marsh Botanical Gardens.

A New Forestry Camp for the University of Maine

Next year's forestry seniors in the University of Maine will have a new woods camp in which to spend the second half of their first semester, according to present plans. Curtis M. Hutchins, formerly a graduate student in the university, has given $1,000 for the purpose of constructing a new permanent camp on condition that the university add a similar amount. It is planned to begin construction of the camp in the spring of this year, on State land near the towns of Princeton and Waite.

Eighteen seniors in the Maine University forestry course attended the winter camp of the present school year, near the town of Grindstone. Prof. R. I. Ashman was in charge of their work, which included study of lumber operations and of silviculture and forest mensuration.

Better Road to Market for Colorado College Forest

In 1931 a new road up Ute Pass having no grades steeper than 6 per cent and having a width such that two heavily loaded trucks can pass anywhere will connect Colorado College's 6,200-acre demonstration forest with Manitou and Colorado Springs, the principal markets for its varied timber products. The old road was double width, but had many sharp turns making it difficult for heavily loaded trucks to pass at any great speed, and had grades as steep as 18 per cent. The improvement of this mountain road and the paving of the 5 miles which were commonly the roughest will permit heavier loads of lumber from the college mill and logs, ties, props, and fuel wood from the forest to be handled with safety and with less wear on the trucks. By reducing hauling costs this will add to the profits of the forest and sawmill and will increase utilization.

Korean Larch Thrives on Manitou Forest

During the past five years the forestry school of Colorado College, at Colorado Springs, has been exchanging forest tree seed with the Korean forest experiment station. Trial sowings and plantings have been made on Manitou Forest, the college's experimental tract, of seed of all the coniferous species of Korea coming from regions having as high altitudes as those of Manitou Forest. The Korean larch has shown exceptional promise and will be used in further experiments. On Manitou Forest plenty of moisture falls during the growing season, but the winters are very dry and many young trees die of winter drought. This larch escapes the danger of winter killing by dropping its needles during the winter, times its needle production during the summer in such a way as to utilize all the favorable weather of the year, and produces a wood having properties not found in the woods of native timber trees.

Forestry in Georgia Rural High Schools

About 20 new agricultural vocational schools started last fall in Georgia are taking up the forestry project begun in the preceding school year by about 100 rural high schools in the State. Each is establishing a school forest, which representatives of the Georgia Forest Service will survey and for which they will make management plans. The school forests are obtained by the schools for practice work under 10-year leases. Demonstrations of tree identification, forest nursery practice, planting, thinning, and timber estimating are conducted on them by the State forest service. On each forest two comparable quarter-acre plots are located side by side, one to be burned over annually and the other to be kept free from fire. Trees on the sample plots are marked with metal tags bearing numbers, and records are kept of their breast-height diameters.

During the past year 40 schools in the State gathered and planted tree seed to grow seedlings for reforestation. More than 50 students started forest-management projects on their home farms.

A prize of $100 was awarded by the Georgia Forestry Association to C. L. Veatch, of Commerce, as the Georgia rural high-school teacher having done the best work in forestry during the year 1929-30.

Forest Recreation Specialist Discusses Camping

Fay Welch, who during the past seven years has directed the Franklin D. Roosevelt Conservation Camps at the Palisades Interstate Park and private camps for children, and who has conducted courses of training in camp leadership for the American Museum of Natural History and for Columbia University, discusses his specialty as follows in a statement sent out from the New York State College of Forestry, where he is engaged in advanced study in forest recreation:

A summer in a good camp is one of the most vital educational experiences for a boy or girl. Here youth is constantly acquiring new skills and interests, developing a sound body, and learning to live on good terms of give and take with other boys and girls and nature herself. There is nothing artificial about the right kind of "lessons" at camp. It is not strange that President Eliot characterized camping as America's most significant contribution to education.

Camp directors are learning that it is wrong to huddle tents or bungalows together. They are also discovering that real camping and forestry activities are more appropriate than town games and indoor occupations. They are finding that to stimulate a constant and feverish competition by means of intricate systems of awards is not conducive to the sound health or stable emotional adjustment of the child.

Winter camping is as interesting as summer camping and, to a robust person who is prepared to meet weather conditions, just as enjoyable. To know the forest and forest life only in summer is to know but half the story. Camping in all seasons is increasing rapidly.

There are some 26,000 camps in the United States accommodating 2,000,000 young people every year. One-third of these lie northeast of a line drawn from Philadelphia to Cleveland.

❧

About 100 North Carolina schools have taken advantage of the offer of the State forest service to supply 1,000 trees without charge to any school that will plant them on its grounds in forest formation. The offer is being continued.

❧

Twenty men were registered for graduate study this year in the New York State College of Forestry. The college's total registration for the first semester was 384.

Farmer Gains by Squirrels' Nut Planting

One of the most attractive agricultural sights along North Carolina Highway No. 10 between Salisbury and Statesville is the 3-acre black walnut grove on the farm of J. G. Lyerly, writes Extension Forester R. W. Graeber; and the trees did not cost their owner even the trouble of planting them. Mr. Lyerly says:

When I located on this farm in 1904 the land now occupied by the walnut grove had been cut over in a lumber operation and was in brush. There was a large bearing walnut tree just to the rear of my home, the only walnut tree on the farm. Near by in some big hollow oaks the squirrels made their homes. Every year I could see the squirrels carrying nuts into the brush to hide them. Many of the nuts were not recovered by the squirrels, and germinated in the spring. I assisted the walnut seedlings by cutting back other sprouts or trees. Many of the trees removed were not cut until they were large enough for fire wood. This field has furnished most of my fire wood for a number of years, and there is yet much to cut. Some of the walnut trees themselves will need to be thinned out where they are crowded. The land is used also as pasture. The nuts harvested have paid the taxes, the fire wood covered interest on investment, the grazing has been my dividends, and the growing crop of walnut timber might be classed as a savings account or an undivided surplus.

Minnesota Farmer and Son Prove that Timber Growing Pays

A "father and son" demonstration of farm forestry as a means of winning returns from poor soil is to be seen on property of a farmer named Vaux, near Faribault, in southern Minnesota, writes Extension Forester Parker O. Anderson. Twenty years ago, after repeated unsuccessful attempts to raise a hay crop on a low, swampy area of 1½ acres, Mr. Vaux planted the area with European white willows three feet apart. Since then he has taken from this small patch hundreds of fence posts, a great deal of material for repairing his farm buildings, and a number of poles which he has sold to neighbors for making sheds. In addition, three years ago the willow plantation provided material for building two log cabins at Roberts Lake. In the fall of 1930 Mr. Vaux planted two bushels of black walnuts and butternuts around the edges of one of his fields.

While still in high school the son, Harold Vaux, started a grove of Norway poplar on a low peat area on the farm. After 13 years these trees are about 14 or 15 inches in diameter and are from 50 to 55 feet high. Thus their yearly growth has averaged about 1 inch in diameter and about 4 feet in height. When one of the trees was cut after 10 years in the field a timber 12 feet long and 8 inches square was obtained from the butt log, and there were two smaller logs. Recently Harold Vaux, who has now had agricultural college training, began planting Carolina poplar on steep hillsides and on sloughs that can not be drained.

35975—31——2

A wild woodland on the Vaux farm has for years provided the family with an annual supply of from 10 to 14 cords of fuel wood. Last year 10,000 feet of oak from this woodlot was sawed into lumber and disposed of locally at $40 per 1,000 feet. The sugar maple from this woodland, sawed into commercial sizes, finds a ready market locally at $75 per 1,000 feet. Basswood and elm also command a very profitable price. In Mr. Vaux's machine shed, stored away to dry, are large boards of walnut, butternut, cherry, oak, elm, maple, poplar, and basswood.

Texarkana Lions Sponsor Forestry Campaign

The Lions Club of Texarkana, Ark.-Tex., has been active for the past two years in efforts to encourage farm forestry, particularly the prevention of woods fires, in its neighborhood. In November, 1930, the club cooperated with county agents and others in arranging a series of forestry meetings in Bowie and Cass Counties, Tex. Eight night meetings were held in schoolhouses. The farm people who gathered at these meetings heard short forestry talks by C. W. Simmons, Texas extension forester; J. R. Thigpen, lecturer of the Texas Forest Service; County Agents W. R. Holsey (Cass County) and C. R. Littlefield (Bowie County); and W. R. Mattoon, extension forester of the United States Forest Service. They saw also the Department of Agriculture films "Friends of Man" and "Pines that Come Back," projected by Mr. Thigpen with apparatus with which the Texas Forest Service has equipped him. Eight field meetings were held, usually on the morning following the schoolhouse meeting and in pine woods in the immediate neighborhood of the schoolhouse. When principles of thinning pine stands had been discussed and illustrated a special measuring card adapted by Mr. Simmons was distributed and its use explained. The farmers and school boys present then competed in estimating the board-foot contents of selected trees. The reward to the individual whose estimate came nearest to that of Mr. Simmons was a double-bitted ax donated by the Lions Club.

Attendance averaged 178 at evening meetings and 38 at woods meetings.

❧

"Soil-saving" demonstrations feature the current program of County Agent Secor in Van Buren County, Iowa. Where good fields are threatened by the washing out of gullies Mr. Secor advises the owners to plant cottonwoods and willows in the bottoms of the gullies and black locusts on the sides and tops. On a number of farms this has been done with pronounced beneficial results. Mr. Secor recommends that the willows and cottonwoods be taken from along rivers and streams, and that the black locusts be raised from the seed in garden rows.

Last year 700 farmers of Custer County, Nebr., planted 250,000 forest trees in cooperation with the extension service, following a special tree-planting campaign launched by County Agent M. L. Gould. In the preceding year only 38,000 trees had been planted in the county in farm forestry projects under extension auspices. All the plantings were for the establishment of windbreaks and shelter belts or for home beautification. As a by-product of the farm plantings, the county superintendent of schools reported, plantings were made on the grounds of 90 per cent of the schools in the county.

※

A circular on the marketing of Illinois forest products has been prepared by Extension Forester L. E. Sawyer for distribution to woodland owners in that State. It lists consumers of forest products in Illinois and in neighboring States.

※

Six 4-H forestry clubs were organized in Idaho in 1930, the first year of 4-H forestry work in that State. The clubs enrolled 104 members. Three of the clubs were formed early enough in the year to complete the first-year project.

Cooperative Selling Increases Christmas-Tree Returns

Twenty farmers in the vicinity of Colebrook, N. H., cooperated this winter in loading and shipping four carloads of Christmas trees, and by so doing obtained about 20 per cent greater returns. This experiment in cooperative marketing was directed by C. S. Herr, extension forester of Lancaster. The 7,200 trees sold, principally balsam fir, were of high quality. A red tag fastened to each tree before it was shipped read "This tree brings a Christmas message from the great outdoors. Its cutting was not destructive, but gave needed room for neighboring trees to grow faster and better." On the reverse the tag bore the name and address of the retailer handling the tree.

※

More than 2,000 specimens of wood from the Peruvian Amazon region were recently added to the Yale School of Forestry's collections. The specimens were collected by L. Williams, assistant in wood technology at the Field Museum of Natural History, and were acquired by the school through exchange with the museum. The Yale wood collections now contain about 19,500 specimens.

Forest Service Notes

Fifty Million Feet of Aspen Sold on Chippewa Forest

By HOWARD HOPKINS, United States Forest Service

About 52,000,000 board feet of aspen timber on the northeast portion of the Chippewa National Forest, Minn., was recently sold by the Government to firms manufacturing box material. The poorer grades will be used for crating; the better grades will go to the packing houses in the form of containers for butter, lard, and other food products, a use for which aspen is especially desirable because of its light weight, whiteness, and freedom from taste or odor. This sale, which includes with the aspen about 13,000,000 board feet of timber of other species, was awarded in two units: One comprising the stumpage on a portion of the Cut Foot Working Circle, the timber from which will go in the main to a mill at Deer River, Minn., on the eastern edge of the forest, and one comprising the stumpage on a portion of the Third River Working Circle, the timber from which will go principally to a mill at Cass Lake, Minn., on the western edge of the forest. A 6-year operation is provided for in the first case, a 10-year operation in the second.

This sale involves the largest body of aspen stumpage ever sold at one time by the Forest Service, and it has several other features of special significance. It is the first large sale in which the Forest Service has availed itself of the provisions of section 3 of the act of June 9, 1930, commonly known as the Knutson-Vandenberg Act. Under this new law governing sales of timber on the national forests, the sale agreement itself makes provision for bringing about the development of an improved stand of timber on the sale area. The law requires that in such sales the buyer shall agree to make a special deposit (which in this instance was fixed at 25 cents per 1,000 board feet of saw timber cut) to provide for the seeding, planting, or cultural improvement of the sale area following the cutting. This removes much uncertainty from Forest Service plans for such work by insuring that the necessary funds will be available and that they will be available at the proper time. In the second place, the sale on the Cut Foot Working Circle represents the first timber sale made on the Chippewa National Forest under an approved timber management plan providing for perpetual sustained yield. The annual cut from this unit is set at from 2,000,000 to 2,500,000 board feet. Finally, the sale agreement will allow very economical scaling. The aspen logs are to be measured by the linear foot and a converting factor applied to ascertain their volume in board feet. This procedure is especially desirable for handling large quantities of low-volume stumpage of uniform cull.

As a result of the Chippewa Forest's steady sustained yield of timber products the towns in its vicinity are among the most prosperous and optimistic in northern Minnesota. The following statement was published editorially in the Cass Lake Times of December 18, 1930:

In 1905 and for years after, the Cass Lake Times was a bitter enemy of the forest policies, for its owners thought with other honest men that the permanent prosperity of this country depended on the stripping off of the forest and the application of the mattock and the plow of the settler and the farmer. In 1905 the Chippewa National Forest did not have a friend among the business men of Cass Lake. To-day the forest not find an out-and-out enemy of its policies. *can* * The forest is the greatest asset that Cass Lake has, and the business men of Cass Lake, without an exception, now realize this very thing.

Lumber Firm Gives Virgin Pine Area to the United States

Twenty acres of highly valuable virgin northern white pine and hemlock land in Forest County, Pa., has been presented to the Government by the lumber-manufacturing firm of Wheeler & Dusenbury. The land is a portion of the Heart's Content area, of which the Government purchased 101 acres from Wheeler & Dusenbury in 1929. Like the purchased land, the gift area will become a part of the Allegheny National Forest. In notifying the donors of the Government's acceptance of the gift C. F. Marvin, Acting Secretary of Agriculture, wrote:

It is planned to maintain this land in a virgin forest condition affected only by such changes as may result from natural organic forces. In this condition it will serve a useful and important purpose as a forest laboratory for the investigation of forest soil problems. At the same time the public will have free access to the area, under such restrictions as will protect it from injury. It is believed that through the medium of this use in contributing to the rebuilding of the white pine forest of the northeastern States, and as an example available to the public of the kind of timber which once clothed this region, the gift will be of greatest benefit to the people of this region and to those of the United States.

Your donation of land is among the first of this kind of any magnitude made by a lumber company to be used for the benefit of research and with the object of promoting a better development of forest lands in the future.

N. P. Wheeler, jr., replying for the donors, wrote:

I know that all those interested in the firm of Wheeler & Dusenbury were glad to make this donation. Those of us actively engaged in the lumber business have a very deep attachment for virgin white pine and have long dreaded the time when the last white pine tree would be cut on this particular logging show.

❦

Quarters for the Intermountain Forest Experiment Station have been leased in the Hotel Bigelow, Ogden, Utah. Director C. L. Forsling now has a technical staff of 1 silviculturist, 1 ecologist, 5 range examiners, and 1 biologist.

National Forest Purchases Approved at Exceptionally Low Price

Meeting December 3, the National Forest Reservation Commission approved the purchase of 257,081 acres of land at an average price of $2.63 per acre. This average price is lower than that of the purchases authorized by the commission in any year of its history. The price is partly explained by the fact that the areas approved for purchase are located largely in the Lake States and in the southern pine regions. Land in 27 purchase units is included in the program.

The commission authorized abandonment of the St. Croix purchase unit in eastern Minnesota, previously approved, and in lieu of it approved the establishment of the Mesaba purchase unit of 181,000 acres, just north of Virginia, Minn., and midway between the Superior and Chippewa National Forests. It also approved additions to the Ocala and Ouachita purchase units, in Florida and Arkansas, respectively, and approved changing the names of the Mackinac and Keweenaw units, in Michigan, to Hiawatha and Ottawa, respectively.

The largest single purchase approved at this meeting is 53,357 acres in the Kiamichi unit, in Oklahoma and Arkansas. The new program covers purchase of 71,306 acres of land in Michigan, 51,885 acres in Florida, 17,939 acres in Minnesota, 19,199 acres in Wisconsin, and smaller areas in Alabama, Georgia, Louisiana, the Carolinas, Virginia, West Virginia, Tennessee, Pennsylvania, New Hampshire, and Maine.

Swift Decay of Douglas Fir Seed on Floor of Virgin Forest

To learn how long Douglas fir seed may lie on the forest floor in the dense shade of virgin timber and remain viable L. A. Isaac, of the Pacific Northwest Forest Experiment Station, recorded for two years the germination of seed so situated, within a rodent-proof inclosure. He sowed 9,000 seed on each of three 4-foot squares. On the first square the seed was sown in spaded soil from which roots had been removed, on the second it was sown on the surface of the duff, and on the third it was placed under a 1-inch layer of duff. At the time when the seed was sown, samples tested were 86 per cent sound and showed a germination of 53 per cent. Within the 2-year period 3.5 per cent of the seed germinated, two-thirds of the germination taking place in the first year. When a sample of the seed remaining at the end of the period was examined none of it was found to be viable. A large proportion of it had germinated sufficiently to crack open, but by far the greater portion had decayed. According to the results of this test Douglas fir seed, to be a factor in restocking forest land following the cutting of old-growth timber, must have fallen within a year or at most two years previous to the time of cutting.

Successful Storage of Longleaf Pine Seed

By PHILIP C. WAKELEY, United States Forest Service

Tests recently completed by the Southern Forest Experiment Station show that successful storage of longleaf pine seed is not impossible or even difficult. Seed stored at low temperatures in tight containers germinated well a year or even two years after collection. Records of the tests are given in the following table:

Crop	Method of storage	Germination per cent		
		Fresh	After 1 year	After 2 years
1927	Sealed glass jars at 25°–30° F.	85	81	82
1928	Friction-top can in ice box, 60°–70° F.	89	75	
1929	Loose-covered cans in fish house, 20°–60° F.	49.2 / 46.8	28.4 / 26.4	

In a commercial nursery test reported to the station, longleaf pine seed that showed a germination percentage of approximately 80 when fresh showed one of approximately 50 after being stored in loose-covered cans at air temperature from November to May and near freezing from May to February.

The figures give some indication that the more tightly covered the containers, the better the result.

In general the germination of cold-storage longleaf pine seed has been as prompt as that of fresh seed, if not prompter.

No other method of storage that has come to the attention of the southern station has so consistently preserved the vitality of longleaf seed. The station recommends that State forestry departments and lumber companies having surplus longleaf pine seed of the current crop put the seed, thoroughly dry, in tightly covered cans and keep it at 32°–35° F. until it is needed for use a year hence. It is expected that the method will work equally well with seed of slash, loblolly, and shortleaf pines.

Florida Pines Bear Hidden Marks of Hurricane

Fifty longleaf pines in western Florida that were cut in 1928 for study by the Forest Products Laboratory did not reveal by the positions in which they were then growing that they been injured by the hurricane of September, 1926. Examination of their wood, however, revealed traces of the hurricane, known to have passed over the region where the trees grew. The annual ring for 1926 showed that growth was normal through most of the growing season of that year; but toward its outer edge appeared compression wood, evidently recording the bent position into which the trees were forced by the hurricane. The formation of compression wood continued through 1927; in 1928 it ceased in some of the trees and became less pronounced in others.

Compression wood is the abnormal type of wood that occurs on the lower sides of leaning trunks of softwood trees and on the under sides of their branches. It is distinguished from normal wood by the relatively greater width of the section of the annual ring in which it occurs, and its summerwood lacks the normal hard, flinty appearance. As seen under the microscope it differs from normal wood in that most of the cells are nearly circular in cross section instead of rectangular or polygonal, and are separated at the corners instead of being completely joined one with another. Its cell walls, also, have spiral checks not present in normal wood. An outstanding characteristic lessening the usefulness of compression wood is the fact that its longitudinal shrinkage is from 3 to 35 times as great as that of normal wood. This excessive shrinkage frequently causes bowing, twisting, and splitting of softwood lumber.

Douglas Fir Forest Intercepts Third of Summer Precipitation

Precipitation measurements made in the open and under a mature stand of Douglas fir during 118 summer showers in the Wind River Valley, Wash., by A. G. Simson, of the Pacific Northwest Forest Experiment Station, indicated that on the average the forest intercepted 34 per cent of the precipitation during these showers. With 8 to 12 gages so distributed that the density of the forest canopy over them ranged from 5 to 95 per cent, 777 measurements were made. The gages used in the open were placed one-half mile from the forest. As shown by the gages in the open, precipitation during the 118 showers ranged from a mere trace to 3.99 inches per shower, and totaled 48.38 inches. The average precipitation per shower was 0.41 inch, and the quantity recorded most often was about 0.04 inch. In the case of light showers, little or none of the precipitation reached the ground under the trees.

With 12 gages placed at 20-foot intervals, checkerboard fashion, 522 additional precipitation measurements were made under a dense 25-year-old Douglas fir stand. These indicated interception of 43 per cent of the summer rainfall. A small portion of this apparent interception, Mr. Simson remarks, was probably accounted for by run-off down the trunks of the trees.

Mr. Simson's report on his findings concludes with the warning: "In the absence of positive knowledge, it is dangerous business for the forest protectionist to assume that a summer shower has caused any significant changes in the fire hazard in the forest itself, regardless of the effect in the open."

A New Undertaking in Tropical Forestry

By J. C. KIRCHER, United States Forest Service

A report on forest conditions in the Virgin Islands prepared by W. P. Kramer, supervisor of the Luquillo National Forest, Porto Rico, in connection with a study of the islands by a commission the chairman of which was Herbert Brown, Chief of the Bureau of Efficiency, has led to a request that the Forest Service undertake some needed forestry work there. Funds for the purpose have been transferred to the Forest Service by the Navy Department. William R. Barbour is returning to the service to take charge of the project under Mr. Kramer's general direction. Since leaving national forest acquisition work in 1918 Mr. Barbour has had tropical forestry experience in Haiti, Santo Domingo, Cuba, Venezuela, British Honduras, and elsewhere. Most recently he has been connected with the Tropical Plant Research Foundation, engaging in explorations of tropical hardwoods. This spring a more thorough survey will be made of forestry problems of the islands and some planting will be done. Planting stock will be obtained from the insular forest nursery at Rio Piedras, P. R.

The hardwood stands which originally covered the Virgin Islands have largely been cut, and much of the forest land is now denuded. The island of St. John still has some second-growth timber and a number of slightly culled areas, but on the other islands of the group a large proportion of the forest area has been taken by brush. St. John is the center of the bay-rum industry, and some bay forests are being grown for this purpose, but the industry has been on the decrease in recent years. The only publicly owned forest land on the islands at present is municipal property totaling about 1,400 acres, which is not under forestry management. According to Mr. Kramer's estimate approximately half the area of the islands, or about 40,000 acres, is suitable only for the production of forest crops. About 20,000 acres of this forest land, he believes, can be brought back to forest growth by protecting it against fire and grazing, but the remainder will need to be planted.

The rapid growth of tropical hardwoods makes it seem practicable to reforest the islands. Such valuable species as mahogany and Spanish cedar would undoubtedly do well on many of the mountain areas. Planted forests would become valuable not only for a much-needed timber supply but also to protect the steeper mountain slopes from erosion and to conserve water supplies.

The Virgin Islands lie about 40 miles east of Porto Rico. Most of the one hundred-odd members of the group are small and uninhabited. The three of greatest importance are St. Croix, with an area of 53,000 acres; St. Thomas, with 16,000 acres; and St. John, with 12,000 acres. The topography of the islands is rolling to rough; their highest peaks rise to 1,500 feet elevation. Temperature is rather even, ranging between 70° and 90° throughout the year. The population, which has been steadily decreasing, is now about 20,000.

Because of their size, the islands do not present an attractive field for national forest extension.

The Inside Story of Slash Pine on Areas Subject to Frequent Fires

By PHILIP C. WAKELEY, United States Forest Service

During the past six years the part played by fire in preventing the establishment and spread of slash pine has been shown strikingly and in detail in St. Tammany Parish, La., on cut-over areas aggregating more than 1,000 acres. The areas lie along the highway and railroad leading to the Bogalusa branch station of the Southern Forest Experiment Station, and have been observed monthly or oftener by members of the southern station staff.

St. Tammany Parish is at the western edge of the natural range of slash pine. Over most of the areas referred to the old-growth stand was longleaf pine; but along each "branch" and in each wet hollow, probably because burning was relatively infrequent in such places, there were a few slash pines. The land between the branches was burned annually or every other year. Logging prior to 1924 left a few small longleaf and slash pine seed trees scattered over the areas.

In the fall of 1924 there was an excellent crop of slash pine seed. There was also a severe drought, which resulted in many early fires. The areas under discussion were for the most part burned over after the seed fell but before it germinated, germination being delayed by the drought. When the seedlings finally started in December and January there was practically no fresh fuel on the ground, and they accordingly escaped being killed by late winter and early spring fires.

In 1926 and in 1927 the areas escaped burning. During this time casual inspection from the highway and the railroad showed no young growth, as the seedlings were still hidden in the tall grass. In the late fall of 1927, however, when the grass turned brown and was matted down by rains, the tops of a good stand of seedlings began to show. By the fall of 1928, from 800 to 1,200 seedlings per acre were well above the grass, spaced almost as evenly as in a plantation and growing thriftily. The Southern Forest Experiment Station had no record of finer reproduction of slash pine anywhere in its territory.

Then came the fires. The first fire got out of control in the winter of 1928–29 during the burning of a railroad right of way and killed most of the seedlings on several hundred acres. The survivors were badly stunted, and succumbed to a second fire the following winter. Other fires in the dry fall of 1929 swept the remaining areas with the exception of one patch. This patch was burned during the severe drought in the spring of 1930.

Now, six years after the seed was shed, nothing remains on all the 1,000 acres but a few hundred scattered, deformed, fire-stunted seedlings. If it were not for the written records kept by the southern station, there would be nothing to show that at one time during the six years the entire 1,000 acres supported a superlatively fine stand of thrifty young slash pines.

Some Effects of Irrigation and Fertilization on the Size of Longleaf Pine Needles

By J. Elton Lodewick,[1] Virginia Polytechnic Institute

Although great strides have been made in the use of irrigation and fertilizers in growing field crops, comparatively little is known as to the effect of such treatment on forest trees. Variation in site conditions may modify a tree's rate of growth, its size and form, and the quality of its wood. Which of the environmental factors related to the soil are operative in producing these modifications is not known.

Several years ago the Forest Products Laboratory started a series of experiments with longleaf pine (*Pinus palustris* Miller) on irrigated and on fertilized sites on the Choctawhatchee National Forest, in western Florida. The investigations were designed primarily to determine what effect variations in the quantities of irrigation water and commercial fertilizers applied would have on the structure of the wood. In each of the first three seasons during which the investigation was under way marked differences in crown density and needle length were observed on certain of the experimental plots. While in charge of this work during the summer of 1928, I attempted to analyze these differences by measurements of a series of needles from each plot, primarily in order to determine whether or not the progression of growth in the needles could be used as an indicator of the efficacy of the various treatments. Though this phase of the investigation was carried on during but one season, and no opportunity for further studies has presented itself, the results may be of use to others as a basis for further investigation.

Apparently but few investigations have been made as to the continued increase in size of the needles of conifers over the period of their retention. Büsgen (*2*) reports that length increments after the first surge of growth result from the activity of a basal meristem. Meissner (*6*) found no characteristic perennial lengthening of the needles in pine, spruce, fir, Douglas fir, or hemlock.

The soil in the region of the Choctawhatchee National Forest is a deep, loose Norfolk sand with a maxi-

mum water-holding capacity of approximately 8 per cent. Not enough organic material is present in or on the soil to call for consideration. Rainfall averages about 60 inches per year and is evenly distributed throughout the vegetative season.

Measurements were made of needles obtained from the lower branches of one tree in each of the eight groups that received a cultural treatment in the experiment. In order to avoid any effect dependent upon vigor due to size, care was taken to select trees as nearly as possible of the same diameter class. In crown density, also, each tree selected represented the average for the group receiving the same treatment. Thus each sample tree was as nearly typical of the group it represented as could be observed. Measurements were made for the most part during late July and early September, 1928. The length of the needles was measured with a scale graduated in millimeters, and the diameters were measured with a micrometer caliper at approximately the middle of each needle. Needle lengthening appeared to have ceased for the season in all trees except those fertilized with a nitrate-potash-sulphate combination.

Preliminary measurements were made in order to determine, if possible, the extent of variation in needle length and diameter on an individual tree. For this purpose a young forest-grown tree 3 inches in diameter and 20 feet tall was selected. The measurements, made in June, 1928, indicate that the needles on the leader, which is more vigorous in growth, are longer than those on the laterals; that the needles increase in length during their second year; and that the more vigorous parts attain a larger proportion of their final length during the first growing season.

While these data were being obtained an apparent relation was observed between the length of needles and their position on the twig. The fascicles were removed and measured in groups of 20 beginning at the base of the current year's growth and progressing toward the apex. It was found that average needle length becomes greater the farther the needles are situated from the base of the year's growth, except that a shorter length is again shown by the last few groups near the apex. The same sequence was noted when leaders from two other trees of comparable size were examined during the fall of 1929. When the data so obtained were plotted there was a marked flattening of the curve at a point slightly beyond the middle. This resembles the flattening noted by Brown (*1*), Friedrich (*3*), Jost (*4*), Mischke (*7*), and Lodewick (*5*) in diameter growth curves of the boles of trees of other species. A retardation of needle growth may occur during the transition period between the formation of spring wood and the formation of summer wood.

Since the data obtained on needle length as correlated with irrigation and with the use of commercial fertilizers are for only one tree under each cultural treatment and for only one season, they are not complete enough to be

[1] Formerly a member of the staff of the U. S. Forest Products Laboratory.

presented in tabular form. The following inferences, however, may be drawn from them. (1) The diameters of the needles were not measurably affected by irrigation or by the use of fertilizers. (2) Irrigation apparently increased the needle length during a dry season. In a year of normal precipitation the water added during irrigation exerted but little influence on the needle length. (3) Trees on fertilized soils showed longer needles than did those on unfertilized sites. The effect was more apparent where a nitrogen-phosphorus mixture had been used than where nitrogen alone had been used. (4) The needles from the trees on the fertilized sites appeared to have had a longer period of growth in length than those on the unfertilized sites.

LITERATURE CITED

1. Brown, H. P.: Growth studies in forest trees. II. Pinus strobus L. Bot. Gaz. 59: 197–241. 1915.

2. Büsgen, M.: Bau und Leben Unserer Waldbäume. Jena, 1917.

3. Friedrich, J.: Über den Einfluss der Witterung auf dem Baumzuwachs. Mittl. Forstl. Versuchs. Oesterr. 22: 160. 1897.

4. Jost, L.: Betrachtungen über den zeitlichen Verlauf des sekundären Dickenwachstum der Bäume. Ber. Deutsch. Bot. Gesells. 10: 587–605. 1892.

5. Lodewick, J. E.: Seasonal activity of the cambium in some northeastern trees. N. Y. State College of Forestry Tech. Pub. 23, 1928.

6. Meissner, R.: Studien über das mehrjährige Wachstum der Kiefernadeln. Bot. Zeitung 1894 und 1897.

7. Mischke, H.: Beobachtungen über das Dickenwachstum der Coniferen. Bot. Centralbl. 44: 39–43; 65–71; 97–102; 137–142; 169–175. 1890.

Storax Production

By ELOISE GERRY, United States Forest Service

Recent news of interest to owners of red gum (*Liquidambar styraciflua* Linnæus) timber is to the effect that there has been an increase in the demand for American-produced storax. Storax (or styrax) is the commercial name for the grayish-brown, sticky, semiliquid substance, known locally as sweet gum, which the red gum tree exudes when wounded. Storax is valued for use in pharmaceutical preparations and adhesives, for incense, for perfuming such products as soap and glove powder, and for flavoring tobacco. For the past two years the quantity imported annually into the United States has exceeded 40,000 pounds. The import prices, for material of widely varying quality, have ranged from $0.40 to $3 per pound. Storax from red gum grown in the United States appears to be as satisfactory for all purposes as the more widely known and used storax from Asia Minor, which is a product of the species Liquidambar orientalis Miller.

Unlike the oleoresin of pines, storax is not present in significant quantities in the normal wood. Its formation is induced by cuts or wounds that expose the surface of the wood beneath the bark. The storax is developed in the new wood that grows when the wound has been made. It exudes from wound resin passages, coating the wood and often soaking into the bark. Preliminary experiments by the Forest Products Laboratory indicated that comparatively small wounds yield more storax than severe ones. Completely girdling a tree resulted in a smaller yield of storax than four approximately horizontal cuts, about ½ inch wide, spaced 4 inches apart, and about 12 feet long altogether.

A microscopical study of specimens taken from the wood surrounding horizontal cuts indicated that the cuts nearer the ground were less productive than those above them. This difference in yield is due not to height on the tree but to the fact that the upper cuts hinder the supply of nutritive material from reaching the lower cuts. It is recommended that not more than two horizontal cuts be made one above the other, and particularly that a vertical bar of about 8 inches of bark be left between pairs of cuts to insure a good opportunity for the circulation of the sap. Cuts should be made low on the butts or on large branches.

The type of scarring described might be further modified by adding vertical cuts, although these are known to be less productive than horizontal cuts of the same length. Tin cans or cups such as are used in turpentining could be used to catch the storax. It is possible that a metal turpentine apron or gutter carefully tacked onto the bark below each cut would reduce the waste that results from the storax soaking into the bark.

Hacks or "hogals" such as those used in the turpentining industry would probably serve best to make the cuts or wounds. Deep cuts are apparently both unnecessary and harmful. All that is needed appears to be a clean cut exposing the outermost layer, or the last year's growth, of the wood. This cut should probably be freshened about every four weeks by removing a shaving about one-half inch thick on the upper side of the cut.

Before shipping the gum the producer usually cleans it by heating it in a double boiler and filtering it through cheesecloth. The collected gum should be kept cool to prevent or reduce fermentation. Shipment can be made in friction-top tin cans.

Trees with decayed hearts or crooked trunks, which will not make good lumber, will often serve well for storax production. Where possible the collection of storax should be made in advance of a lumbering operation, so that the scarred trees need not stand for any great length of time exposed to insect or fungus attack. Among the hardwood species cut in the South, red gum ranks second only to the oaks. It composes about 25 per cent of the total annual cut of hardwoods in the United States, and about 2 per cent of the total cut of all species. On large tracts where red gum makes up 15 to 50 per cent of the timber cut it should be possible to combine storax production with cutting. Where trees are scattered and are not highly valued for lumber, farmers or high-school boys or others may be able to carry on small-scale operations during their spare time, for storax is purchased in lots as small as 4 pounds each.

The yield obtained in Louisiana from the horizontal wounds described in the foregoing averaged 2.5 ounces per tree per year. Total girdling of trees gave a yield of only 1.5 ounces for each tree. The highest yields are said to be obtained in the warmer regions and in the warmer seasons.

Further experiments are needed to determine optimum conditions for storax production. Until more is known about all angles of the problem great care should be taken not to damage valuable timber through wounding it to obtain storax.

Seed Collection of 1930 in Northern Rocky Mountains

Western white pine seed collected and extracted on the Kaniksu National Forest, Wash.-Idaho, in the fall of 1930 cost the Forest Service $2.14 a pound. In the preceding 15 years the cost to the service of collecting and extracting seed of this species averaged about $3.50 a pound. The low cost in 1930 was due principally to good yield from the cones and efficient operation of the seed extractory. The regular price of 75 cents a sack was paid for the cones. On the average each sack of cones yielded .88 pound of seed. The cost per pound of seed included 86 cents for cone collection, 78 cents for extraction work, and 50 cents depreciation on improvements and equipment. About 600 pounds of seed was collected.

An unusually complete and ample 3-year supply of seed of the more important forest tree species of the northern Rocky Mountain region was collected in 1930 by national forest officers for use in local reforestation projects.

[CORRECTION: Seed-crop observations of Jacob Roeser, jr., quoted on page 14 of the FOREST WORKER of November, 1930, had as their field not the northern Rocky Mountain region (Montana, northern Idaho, etc.) but the Rocky Mountain region (Wyoming, Colorado, etc.).]

The one-fourth share of national forest receipts which by law goes to the counties containing the forests, to be used for roads and schools, amounted for the fiscal year 1930 to $1,677,559. It was divided among 28 States, Alaska, and Porto Rico. The one-tenth share available to the Forest Service for constructing roads and trails on the national forests amounted for the year to $671,023.

General Forest News

Use of Plows and Pumps for Fire Fighting in the Douglas Fir Region

By C. S. COWAN, Washington Forest Fire Association

Before caterpillar tractors and plows could be introduced as forest fire fighting equipment in the Douglas fir region it was necessary to devise a special type of plow. The plow developed for use in the pine regions of Oregon, California, and Washington, where the caterpillar tractor and plow were introduced as firefighting apparatus some time ago, was found unsuitable to the rougher Douglas fir type of country, with its heavy litter, dense stands of timber or stumps, and heavy slash. The Killifer "pan buster," a 2-faced plow used in digging irrigation ditches, proved to be badly placed for fire fighting purposes, and its carriage frame and wheels were not equal to the tremendous strains placed upon them by the work of making fire trails in rugged country. The pan buster served, however, as the model on which a suitable plow was finally developed. Two plow blades formed of boiler plate were welded to a gooseneck of 60-pound railroad steel, which was reinforced between the web and the flange. The gooseneck carried the point of the plow some 30 inches behind the wheels. The placing of the plow to the rear prevented clogging between the plow proper and the wheels. The wheels themselves were reinforced with 3-inch channel iron, which kept them round and kept the (iron) spokes in place. The frame, which developed a tendency to spread under long pulling strains, was effectively strengthened with a brace welded from one side to the other.

A 15 caterpillar tractor was found to be best adapted to work in the Douglas fir country so far as concerns the Washington Forest Fire Association, which in getting its fire equipment to the scene of action has to transport it over long distances. For general work it was found advisable to place a stout metal tool box upon one of the fenders of the tractor and to reinforce both fenders. In the tool box were carried two blocks with 5-inch sheaves, and two wire rope straps. On the rear of the tractor was attached a reel with 175 feet of soft steel wire rope, together with a choker. This made it possible to move logs and down trees without bucking, and helped in swamping out the line as a preliminary to the actual trail building.

It was found that one caterpillar tractor and plow with a crew of two (one to drive and one to ride the plow), plus a swamping crew ranging from four to eight, according to the type of ground cover, could build from 3 to 4 miles of excellent fire trail per day. This trail was distinctly better than a handmade trail. The plow action left plenty of loose earth available to be shoveled onto the fire, whereas a handmade trail simply exposes the mineral soil. It appears further that the "cat"-made trail, instead of disappearing or becoming useless in one year as a handmade trail often does, will last for several years. Roots of living trees up to 3 inches in diameter offered little resistance to the plow and tractor.

Next came the problem of transportation. The cost of a truck to transport such a piece of equipment, weighing around 5,000 pounds, may easily exceed the cost of the equipment itself. A low-bed truck was sought, with the purpose of keeping the weight close to the ground and obviating the risk of accidents in connection with the loading and unloading operations. The one chosen was the Golden State Lo Bed truck, an assembled truck with a Ford power plant plus a strong capable body carrying its own system of transmission, with braking power fully up to requirements. The cooling system was found inadequate, but addition of a 4-gallon auxiliary water tank above the power plant put this matter in order. The cost of this truck was about half that of a standard low-bed truck with sufficient weight-carrying capacity. In view of the small mileage run annually, all requirements as to performance were met.

The usefulness of the equipment has been proved beyond all doubt. By increasing the speed of trail building it reduces acreage burned over; it builds better trail; and it reduces man-power requirements and, therefore, reduces fire-fighting costs and damage. There is the further point that not so many shovels, mattocks, axes, and other hand tools disappear as under the old system of fire-line building.

This outfit does not completely meet the fire-line construction needs of the Douglas fir region, of course; on most fires in the region it can not be used, because of topography, density of débris, etc. But it can be used in a greater proportion of cases than was originally thought possible, and it is sufficiently successful to warrant the purchase of additional equipment of a similar nature. Such purchase is planned both by the State and by the Washington Forest Fire Association.

The usefulness of pumps in fire fighting is already well tested. We believe in having available in large numbers a light-weight pump such as can be carried by one man. In the operation of pumps much depends upon the operator. The type of pumps in general use in this association is the Pacific Marine, which as a rule gives very little trouble if treated with average care.

Some years ago the British Columbia Forest Service experimented with a universal type of hose connection. While an improvement on the screw type of connection, this was not altogether satisfactory. During 1930 the Washington Forest Fire Association, working in conjunction with the Seattle Brass Co., evolved a universal coupling patterned somewhat upon the type tried out in British Columbia which apparently remedies

all the defects found in that type. This coupling, shown in the accompanying drawing, requires but an inch turn to make connections, is absolutely watertight, and has the advantage of utilizing the water pressure in such a way as to become tighter with every

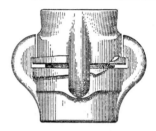

pound of pressure increase. It can be used for all connections. It can always be connected with standard screw type connections through an adapter carried upon the nozzle. As compared with screw couplings it saves some 20 minutes in connecting 1,000 feet of hose. This universal coupling met with instant approval of the field men in our force. Some 80,000 feet of hose was equipped with it, and not a single complaint has been received as to its efficiency. To our minds, this is the greatest advance brought out in recent years in type of connections. We confidently expect to see it adopted by other fire-fighting organizations.

In hose construction little advance has been made. The rubber-lined cotton hose commonly used in forest fire fighting is far too heavy to give satisfaction in the Douglas fir country. It would appear that here is an opening for a progressive hose manufacturer.

❦

A film strip entitled "Preventing Termite Damage, Series 260," is available for distribution by the Department of Agriculture. The film strip and a 7-page lecture accompanying it can be obtained at a charge of 35 cents from the Office of Cooperative Extension Work, United States Department of Agriculture, Washington, D. C.

❦

The gypsy-moth laboratory of the United States Bureau of Entomology at Melrose Highlands, Mass., has moved from 17 East Highland Avenue to 1156 Main Street.

❦

Deer killed by hunters in California in the 1930 season numbered 24,131, the State division of fish and game reports. This number exceeds the 1929 kill by 14 per cent.

Society of American Foresters Meets

More than 300 members of the Society of American Foresters gathered in Washington, D. C., for the society's annual meeting in the closing three days of 1930. The meeting marked the passage of 30 years since the society was first formed by a group of seven men, Gifford Pinchot, O. W. Price, W. L. Hall, Ralph Hosmer, Thomas Sherrard, E. T. Allen, and Henry S. Graves. The society's membership is now 1,740.

In opening the meeting with a review of forestry activities and events of the past year President Paul G. Redington spoke particularly of the advantages which the society had gained through creating the full-time position of executive secretary and through obtaining the services of W. R. Hine in that position.

Practitioners of private forestry on a commercial scale held the floor in the opening session of the meeting, with William L. Hall, of Hall, Kellogg & Co., in the chair. Julian E. Rothery, of the International Paper Co., spoke on "the economic approach to forest management." A paper on the management of southern pine for naval stores by I. F. Eldredge, of the Superior Pine Products Co., Georgia, was read. Ernest F. Jones, forester of the Great Northern Paper Co., Bangor, Me., outlined current forestry conceptions of timberland owners in the Northeast spruce region. In that region, Mr. Jones told the society, the adoption of "orthodox" forestry practices such as timber marking is deferred by the uncertainty of adequate returns on the investment involved; but there is no real devastation by logging, fire protection has a creditable record extending back over 20 years, utilization is close, and more trained foresters are employed than in any other region of the same size in North America. Russell Watson, of Banzháf & Watson (Inc.), Milwaukee consulting foresters, spoke of private forestry in the Lake States. Mr. Watson stated that he knows of no lumber company in the Lake States, "sawing logs and marketing lumber for a living," that plans on a perpetual forestry operation; but that the pulp and paper companies, he is satisfied, will steadily build up permanent producing forests contiguous to their plants. Mr. Watson dwelt especially on the attractive opportunities in the Lake States for independent forestry ventures by foresters. He and his partner, after practicing timber growing for several years as a side line, now make it their principal activity. Suggesting that there is no particular way to explain why more foresters do not practice independently what they learned in school, aside from the fact that "they don't seem to think of it," Mr. Watson concluded "It is an obviously simple thing to do; it offers a lot more fun and is more profitable than most foresters' jobs."

The public land policy of the United States was the subject of an afternoon symposium, in which it was brought out that many of the Western States do not desire transfer to them of public domain lands.

At the society's thirtieth anniversary banquet, with Dean H. S. Graves as toastmaster, greetings from foresters of Canada, of Great Britain, of France, and of Switzerland, respectively, were brought to the society by Ellwood Wilson, of the Canadian Society of Forest Engineers; W. E. Hiley, of the Imperial Forestry Institute, Oxford; Louis Duplaquet, inspecteur-adjoint des eaux et forêts, Nancy; and J. W. Zehnder, of the Swiss Society of Foresters. The "American epic" of the 30-year growth of the movement for forest conservation was ably narrated by Raphael Zon. (Through permission granted to Hon. Scott Leavitt, of Montana, Mr. Zon's address was printed in the Congressional Record of January 5, pp. 1446–1448.)

On the second morning a survey of the field of the profession of forestry culminated in "a look ahead" by Dean Graves. After a period of preparation prior to 1900, said the dean, American forestry has now entered a second period in which the obligations of the public in forestry are being recognized, national, State, and other public forests are being established, and other activities such as organized fire protection, reform of taxation, and work in research and education are being carried forward. History suggests that we may anticipate a third period marked by the initiation on a substantial scale of forestry on private lands, and a fourth period representing the maturing of the whole enterprise, with the stabilizing of economic conditions which will permit a progressive intensification of forestry practice. Dean Graves foresees a very material expansion of public forestry within the next 10 years. As factors justifying this expectation he lists the problems of land utilization and public finance presented to States and counties by the reversion of land for tax delinquency; the growing problem of conserving waters and controlling their flow; growing appreciation of the public loss caused by present wasteful liquidation of some of our natural resources; and the tremendous sweep of the forces behind the recreation movement. For the near future he anticipates a new step forward in fire protection. He believes that forestry work in all its branches will become increasingly exacting as regards technical knowledge and proficiency, a prospect calling for correction of serious deficiencies in the forestry educational system of the present.

Some of the information back of Dean Graves's remarks on the forestry educational situation was brought out when C. H. Guise presented a progress report of the committee on forestry education. Most of the field work involved in the study begun by the committee in July, 1929, has now been completed, and it is hoped to complete next summer a report covering conditions in all the forestry schools of the United States.

Following the report of the committee on industrial forestry, presented by Shirley W. Allen, it was decided to continue the work of the committee, which is in the nature of a census of industrial concerns practicing forestry.

Technical papers read at the meeting, which are being published in the Journal of Forestry, were the following: The management of shortleaf and loblolly pine for saw timber, by A. E. Wackerman, Crossett Lumber Co.; Chemical utilization of wood waste, by L. F. Hawley, Forest Products Laboratory; Forest fire protection, by S. B. Show, United States Forest Service; The white pine blister rust in the Inland Empire, by S. B. Detwiler, Bureau of Plant Industry; The effect of defoliation on tamarack, by S. A. Graham, University of Michigan; Erosion, by E. I. Kotok, United States Forest Service; and Reforestation of abandoned farm lands in New York State, by Duncan G. Rankin, New York State Conservation Commission.

Measures urged in the resolutions adopted by the society include adequate provision by Congress for enlargement of the Federal program of research in erosion control and streamflow regulation and for control of the gypsy moth; provision by Congress and by the States and private landowners for immediate and adequate steps to control the white pine blister rust; preservation of a primitive area of the Florida Everglades as a national park; the conferring of a definite legal status as "Indian forests" on all unallotted lands within Indian reservations that may be found to be primarily adapted to the production of forest crops, needed for purposes of water conservation, or essentially contributory to the prevention of soil erosion; establishment of a foreign agricultural service under which it would be possible to send a forester abroad to keep American foresters in touch with European developments; and action by State legislatures to make emergency funds available for forestry work on State-owned lands as a measure for relief of unemployment.

Following adjournment, many members of the society witnessed a field demonstration of the Champion reforesting machine, the rototiller firebreak-cutting machine, and caterpillar tractors, arranged by State Forester Besley of Maryland and his staff.

Bryce Canyon Park Enlarged

Bryce Canyon National Park, in southwestern Utah, is more than doubled in area by a presidential proclamation of January 5, 1931. To the 14,480 acres of the park area as formerly established 16,080 acres are added by transfer from the Powell National Forest. The addition includes a crescent of eroded area in the Pink Cliffs that is 8 miles from tip to tip. One point in the newly added territory gives an unobstructed view over an arc of 320°. From this point, on a clear day, it is possible to see mountain ranges in the five States of Utah, Arizona, Colorado, New Mexico, and Nevada.

When Douglas Found the Sugar Pine

[From journal kept by David Douglas during his travels in North America, 1823-1827]

THURSDAY, Oct. 26, 1826.—Weather dull and cloudy. When my people in England are made acquainted with my travels, they may perhaps think I have told them nothing but my miseries. That may be very correct, but I now know that such objects as I am in quest of are not obtained without a share of labour, anxiety of mind, and sometimes risk of personal safety. I left my camp this morning at daylight on an excursion, leaving my guide to take care of the camp and horses until my return in the evening, when I found everything as I wished; in the interval he had dried my wet paper as I desired him. About an hour's walk from my camp I was met by an Indian, who on discovering me strung his bow and placed on his left arm a sleeve of raccoon-skin and stood ready on the defence. As I was well convinced this was prompted through fear, he never before having seen such a being, I laid my gun at my feet on the ground and waved my hand for him to come to me, which he did with great caution. I made him place his bow and quiver beside my gun, and then struck a light and gave him to smoke and a few beads. With my pencil I made a rough sketch of the cone and pine I wanted and showed him it, when he instantly pointed to the hills about fifteen or twenty miles to the south. As I wanted to go in that direction, he seemingly with much good-will went with me. At midday I reached my long-wished *Pinus* (called by the Umpqua tribe *Natele*), and lost no time in examining and endeavoring to collect specimens and seeds. New or strange things seldom fail to make great impressions, and often at first we are liable to over-rate them; and lest I should never see my friends to tell them verbally of this most beautiful and immensely large tree, I now state the dimensions of the largest one I could find that was blown down by the wind: Three feet from the ground, 57 feet 9 inches in circumference; 134 feet from the ground, 17 feet 5 inches; extreme length, 215 feet. The trees are remarkably straight; bark uncommonly smooth for such large timber, of a whitish or light brown colour, and yields a great quantity of gum of a bright amber colour. The large trees are destitute of branches, generally for two-thirds the length of the tree; branches pendulous, and the cones hanging from their points like small sugar-loaves in a grocer's shop, it being only on the very largest trees that cones are seen, and the putting myself in possession of three cones (all I could) nearly brought my life to an end. Being unable to climb or hew down any, I took my gun and was busy clipping them from the branches with ball when eight Indians came at the report of my gun. They were all painted with red earth, armed with bows, arrows, spears of bone, and flint knives, and seemed to me anything but friendly. I endeavored to explain to them what I wanted and they seemed satisfied and sat down to smoke, but had no sooner done so than I perceived one string his bow and another sharpen his flint knife with a pair of wooden pincers and hang it on the wrist of the right hand, which gave me ample testimony of their inclination. To save myself I could not do by flight, and without any hesitation I went backwards six paces and cocked my gun, and then pulled from my belt one of my pistols, which I held in my left hand. I was determined to fight for life. As I as much as possible endeavored to preserve my coolness and perhaps did so, I stood eight or ten minutes looking at them and they at me without a word passing, till one at last, who seemed to be the leader, made a sign for tobacco, which I said they should get on condition of going and fetching me some cones. They went, and as soon as out of sight I picked up my three cones and a few twigs, and made a quick retreat to my camp, which I gained at dusk. The Indian who undertook to be my last guide I sent off, lest he should betray me. Wood of the pine fine, and very heavy; leaves short, in five, with a very short sheath bright green; cones, one 14½ inches long, one 14, and one 13½, and all containing fine seed. A little before this the cones are gathered by the Indians, roasted on the embers, quartered, and the seeds shaken out, which are then dried before the fire and pounded into a sort of flour, and sometimes eaten round [sic]. How irksome a night is to such a one as me under my circumstances! Can not speak a word to my guide, not a book to read, constantly in expectation of an attack, and the position I am now in is lying on the grass with my gun beside me; writing by the light of my Columbian candle—namely, a piece of wood containing rosin.

New Bird Refuges Created

Land purchases authorized by the Migratory Bird Conservation Commission on December 18, 1930, will add four units to the series of sanctuaries for which provision was made in the migratory bird conservation act of 1929. A unit along Apalachee Bay, Fla., to be known as the St. Marks Migratory Bird Refuge, contains 13,981 acres. A purchase in California will add 8,982 acres to the Salton Sea Wild Life Refuge, created by an Executive order of November on 15,733 acres of lands in Imperial County, Calif., that are included in the Yuma reclamation project. The Swanquarter Migratory Bird Refuge will be established in North Carolina, on 11,778 acres in Hyde County, on Pamlico Sound, which together with intermingled water areas will make an administrative unit of about 20,000 acres. Purchase of a 39,038-acre sandhill area in Garden County, Nebr., will result in the creation of the Crescent Lake Migratory Bird Refuge.

Units previously approved for purchase or otherwise established as migratory bird refuges under the 1929 law have an aggregate area of 84,387 acres, so that the addition of the units just listed makes the total 158,167 acres.

Quick Poison for Poison Ivy

A poison for undesired plants, such as poison ivy or poison oak, that acts quickly and surely and then clears out of the soil was recently described before the American Society of Plant Physiologists by R. B. Harvey, of the University of Minnesota. It is ethylene oxide, chemically related to the ethylene chloride which has been found to hasten very effectively the ripening of fruits and vegetables. Professor Harvey tried the compound on some large barberry bushes, marked for destruction because the plant harbors the black stem rust of wheat. "Depth charges" of ethylene oxide dissolved in water were sunk into holes pierced in the soil at the roots of the bushes. A few days later every one of the treated bushes was found to be in the last stages of the death struggle. About 1½ ounces of ethylene oxide diluted to a 10 per cent solution in water sufficed for a large bush.

❧

An unusual demonstration of the rapidity of growth of slash pine planted in Washington Parish, La., is reported by Philip C. Wakeley, of the Southern Forest Experiment Station. Twice during the summer of 1930 armed bandits robbed the bank at Angie, La., some miles north of Bogalusa, and fled toward Varnado and Bogalusa. Each time, upon finding themselves closely pursued they abandoned their car and took refuge on foot in a large plantation of slash pine established in the spring of 1926 on lands of the Great Southern Lumber Co. The area is flat and almost devoid of brush, but the shelter of the planted pines enabled the robbers to make good their escape. The trees, 5½ years old from seed and 4½ years in the field, are now about 10 feet high.

❧

Chilling on ice hastened the germination of the large edible seed of pines native to California in experiments carried out by botanists of the University of Southern California. For the highest percentages of germination Torrey pine seed from the Torrey Pine Preserve near La Jolla required 25 days of chilling and seed of Digger and Coulter pines required 50 and 60 days, respectively. Experiments with seed of the single-leaf piñon indicated that seed of this species germinate best after 30 days on ice.

❧

Visitors to the national parks again increased in number last year, reports Horace M. Albright, director of the National Park Service. In the 1930 travel year, ending September 30, the parks were visited by 2,818,618 persons. Yosemite and Mount Rainier National Parks had 458,566 and 265,620 visitors, respectively.

Foreign Notes

Something New in Forest Planting

By BERT R. LEXEN, United States Forest Service

The Norwegian forestry journal Skogbrukeren announces the advent of a new forest planting machine, the announcement bearing the rather enthusiastic title "An international planting method." The machine is an invention of the Norwegian forester Aksel Bakken. Bakken some time ago conceived the idea of planting forest tree seed in small squares of sod that could be set out in the field during the seedling stage without any particular reference to the planting season. This idea has materialized as a machine that, when fed with seed and with a suitable mixture of soil and moisture, automatically forms a soil briquet, pokes a hole in it, drops in two or three seed, sprinkles soil over the seed, and then gently presses the soil layer down. (The drawing accompanying the description suggests that the briquet is about 2 by 2 by 5 inches.) After this operation a claw lifts the briquet forward and dips it into a solution of paraffin, which serves to hold the briquet intact until it is finally planted. The briquets can be stored almost anywhere in the open until a year after germination, when they are ready to be set out on the planting area. In one year the roots of some of the seedlings grown by this method developed so far that they began to protrude from the sides of the briquet.

At present the machine can produce 16,000 briquets in an 8-hour day. With later improvements it is expected to increase this figure, although an output of approximately one briquet every two seconds is astounding enough. Certainly, the method is a great advance on the old form of ball planting.

In developing the mechanical features of the machine Bakken enlisted the aid of a well-known Norwegian machine designer, Birger Holm-Hansen. The first machine was turned out in a German factory last summer. A company has been formed with an actual capital of approximately $134,000 to develop the method and set it out on the world market. Present plans call for introducing it first in England and later in other countries.

The machine-made soil briquet promises to become an important factor in forest planting. In much of our planting in the United States the difficulty of handling the briquets on the planting areas would be considerable, because of their bulk and fragility; but that one difficulty may be greatly overbalanced by the many advantages of this method of planting. This method prolongs the planting season almost indefinitely, eliminates the expense of transplanting the seedlings and later cultivating them, reduces root disturbance to the minimum and thus tends to bring about better survival, gives the maximum opportunity for development of a good root system (something that is not always assured by present planting methods) and enhances the possibility of success in propagating some of the more delicate species and in planting on adverse sites.

Provincial Forest Services Created in Prairie Provinces of Canada

Manitoba, Saskatchewan, and Alberta each have a new provincial forest service, recently created in consequence of the transfer of responsibility for administration of natural resources from the Dominion Government to the provincial governments. Through this change the Dominion forest service has become primarily a research rather than an administrative organization. The new provincial foresters are H. I. Stevenson, E. H. Roberts, and T. F. Blefegen. All these men have had long experience as officers of the Dominion forest service in their respective Provinces.

Forest Management Enters Second Decade in Western Australia

In the year ending with June, 1930, forest improvement work in Western Australia for the first time covered an area greater than the forest area cut over during the year, the State's forests department reports. On 49,395 acres of indigenous forest, principally jarrah, measures were taken for the protection, development, and improvement of natural regrowth; from 44,700 acres, 29,382,233 cubic feet of timber was extracted. The year began the second decade of forest management in Western Australia. In the 1929 planting season the area of pine plantations was increased by 791 acres, bringing the total to 4,061 acres. Pinus radiata and Pinus pinaster again formed the main portion of the planting stock used; but 126 acres of experimental plantations were established with Pinus canariensis, P. palustris, P. longifolia, P. laricio, P. taeda, P. caribaea, P. jeffreyi, P. coulteri, P. banksiana, P. ponderosa, and other conifers. An increase of 39,000 pounds in exports of sandalwood oil brought the year's total to the record figure of 131,400 pounds. Termite investigations and a study of preservative treatment of fence posts were continued during the year, and a bulletin was published on air seasoning of jarrah flooring.

Australia Establishes Commonwealth Forestry Bureau

Establishment of a Commonwealth forestry bureau in Australia is provided for by a recent act of the Federal parliament. The bureau is to be under the charge of the inspector general of forests. Its powers and functions will include advising the territorial governments on all matters pertaining to the management of forests; managing forests placed under its control by the Governor General; establishing experiment stations for the study of silviculture, forest management, and forest protection; providing educational facilities for the training of professional foresters; establishing and awarding forestry scholarships; collecting and distributing forestry information; and publishing reports and bulletins dealing with forestry.

The same act establishes a "forestry fund" which the inspector general of forests, the secretary to the treasury, and the secretary to the department of home affairs will control as trustees. This provides for the administration of such gifts to the Commonwealth as that of £5,000 made in 1929 by Russell Grimwade, of Melbourne. Mr. Grimwade's gift sustains a traveling scholarship in forestry, tenable for one year, open to graduate foresters with two years' experience in the Commonwealth forestry service or that of one of the States.

Forest Fire Insurance in France

Mutual forest fire insurance organizations were founded in 1928 in three departments of the central plateau region of France, where considerable reforestation is under way and where the danger of serious fires is slight because of favorable climate and scattered distribution of woodlands. In 1929 these organizations joined in a regional association for reinsurance. Insurance is written principally on young stands and covers the value of the trees only. The maximum single risk is 230,000 francs. Contracts run for five years. Premium rates range from 0.5 to 2.5 per mille on broadleaf stands and from 0.5 to 1.2 per mille on conifers, according to age. If funds are available, rebates are paid to members who have taken special measures to protect their forests and who have had no fires.

℞

Areas under teak in Java at present total 1,897,000 acres, reports Assistant Trade Commissioner Warren S. Lockwood, Batavia. Other forest reserves, including certain areas in need of reforestation, total 4,088,000 acres. Other forests, of which it is expected that part will be annexed to the forest reserve and part turned to agricultural use, cover 1,420,000 acres.

Twisted Fiber in Pinus Longifolia

After a 4-year interval H. G. Champion, silviculturist of the Forest Research Institute of India, has again reported on an inspection of plots of Pinus longifolia grown in Kumaon from selected seed in order to study the cause of twisted fiber (Mr. Champion's conclusions from an earlier inspection were quoted on page 17 of the FOREST WORKER of January, 1928.) At the time of the recent inspection the plants were mostly 13 and 14 years old and it was possible "to collect most of the data at breast height instead of near ground level, and so to bridge the gap that has hitherto existed between the seedling and the sapling and small pole stages." Mr. Champion's deductions from the 1930 data, and the application he suggests, are as follows:

The chief conclusion, which it is ventured to suggest, is established beyond possible further doubt, is that the production of twisted fiber is a character which is inherited from one generation to the next, independently of any influence which soil and treatment may exert.

It can not be asserted that a 100 per cent twisted parent crop will give a 100 per cent twisted second rotation crop from natural regeneration, whether it is protected from adverse external influences or not, but it can be stated already that about two-thirds at least will be twisted beyond serviceability for timber, even given that complete protection which experience has proved impossible in present practice. There are indications that the usual damage from trampling and burning may increase this percentage.

The use of imported seed from a suitable source will give a crop at least to the sapling stage which is virtually free of twist, even in localities where the original crop is 100 per cent twisted.

The use of seed from straight trees in localities in which the percentage of twist is moderate or low will similarly give crops in which the percentage of twisted stems will not exceed about 25 per cent, and may perhaps be comparable with the parent crop.

The use of seed from straight trees growing among a twisted crop is definitely preferable to that of seed from twisted parent trees growing among a predominantly straight crop, and may result in a new crop about 40 per cent twisted as compared with 60 per cent for the latter.

Closely comparable results are obtained in three of the four localities, demonstrating independence of soil, underlying rock, and aspect. (The fact that the fourth locality, Kaligadh, has given definitely lower percentages of twisted stems with both types of seed used and is also the locality with the least twist in the existing crops is noteworthy and may be important, but unfortunately the figures have not the same weight as those from the other localities, being based on small numbers of measurements, obtaining no further support from data of other years, and the seed used being from supposedly comparable but actually different sources.)

The results agree throughout with those obtained in 1926 and 1923 and so derive additional reliability, particularly where the numbers of trees now measured are small.

The tentative conclusion is confirmed, which was reached on the data available up to 1921, that left-handed twist in Pinus longifolia in Kumaon is of the nature of a Mendelian dominant character which has originated independently in many localities, its extension being due to the long-continued selection of the straighter trees for removal.

More confidently even than in 1926, it must be stressed that for all artificial regeneration work careful selection of seed is a matter of utmost importance. It would be preferable to import from Naini Tal, Chakrata, or other similar localities all the seed required, and with the cheap motor transport now available this can not be ruled out as totally impracticable. As, however, the bulk of the seed required must probably still be obtained locally, the need of strict insistence on the use of seed from straight trees is clear. The obvious source of seed is the main timber fellings, and if it is still found that the fellings are usually done too early in the season for the seed to be fertile (the valuable information that the cones can safely be collected as soon as they are full sized in December—*vide* S. H. Howard, Chir Seed Supply, For. Bull. No. 67—is still not generally utilized, it is believed), then, as has been found both necessary and practical in several other types of forest, the time of felling must be altered.

In making regeneration fellings in mature crops with a good proportion of straight trees, the straight trees must be selected as seed bearers even at the sacrifice of good spacing.

In making regeneration fellings in mature crops with a high proportion of twisted trees a very marked improvement may be looked for if the seed trees are mainly straight. The proportion twisted in the second rotation may be half that in the first.

The retention of unfit marked trees in shelterwood regeneration fellings, on the score of cost of felling, is strongly condemned as contrary to all the tenets of good silviculture and in the face of the clear proofs now available of the results on the regeneration. These trees have to be felled sooner or later, and it should emphatically be sooner.

The treatment of advance growth in areas brought under regeneration must be considered in the light of the foregoing paragraphs, which show what may be expected. It should be examined for twist in any case, and only retained if up to the standard probably attainable with the given parent crop.

While a good deal more evidence is still required, the experience gained in the 14 years' course of these investigations all goes to indicate that the ordinary forms of injury to which *chir* regeneration is subjected—burning, browsing, trampling, etc.—are not factors of first importance in the development of twisted fiber, though by causing distortion of the stem they may exaggerate the defect already present.

❦

Forest and Outdoors, the monthly magazine published by the Canadian Forestry Association, goes into 12,000 schools to be used in teaching conservation. For schools the annual subscription price is $1, less than cost. Prizes totaling $65, and 25 annual subscriptions, were recently awarded by the association to rural school teachers for lesson plans based on material in the magazine. Material from the magazine is regularly reproduced by 450 newspaper editors in Canada.

Yellow Poplar Withstands Extreme Cold in Ukraine

Yellow poplar has a good chance of successful introduction into southern Ukraine, foresters of the Vesselo-Bokovenkovska Dendrological Experiment Station concluded on the basis of the frost resistance which the tree exhibited at that station in the early months of 1929. The station is located at 48° 10' north latitude in a dry prairie region in the southwest of the Union of Socialist Soviet Republics. Exotic trees and shrubs growing there passed through a very severe test in 1929, when temperatures as low as $-35°$ C. were recorded. The yellow poplars, which were 21 years old or older, endured this ordeal without greater injury than freezing back of twigs of the previous year's growth to a distance of not more than 12 inches from the tips.

High Latitudes Temper Sun's Rays to the Unshaded Seedling

Discussing the danger to unshaded tree seedlings of death due to overheating at the soil surface, W. E. Hiley, of the Imperial Forestry Institute, Oxford University, has called attention as follows to an advantage enjoyed by Swedish silviculture:

The cheapest method of regeneration, which frequently proves successful in Sweden, is to leave scattered mother trees, singly or in clumps, from which the surrounding almost bare areas may be naturally seeded. In Sweden they appear to have little trouble from high soil-surface temperatures and can adopt this method which in southern Germany would generally fail. We must remember, however, that the temperature of the surface soil under direct insolation is determined principally by the angle of incidence of the sun's rays. In Sweden, at a latitude of 60°, this can never be more than 38°, whereas in Quebec at a latitude of 45° to 50° it is very much higher; and I have observed in Quebec that on bare ground coniferous seedlings only succeed in establishing themselves on the north side of boulders and logs. This suggests that in Quebec methods of natural regeneration will have to follow the practice of southern Germany rather than Sweden.

❦

Among Canadian trees those to which the 1930 drought proved most disastrous were the willows and the Manitoba maple, with the poplars next, says the Canadian Forestry Association. White spruce, ash, and elm appeared to suffer very little. Caragana demonstrated exceptional ability to withstand adverse conditions.

❦

Plant-quarantine regulations in force in the Union of South Africa prohibit importation of Eucalyptus, acacia, or any conifers.

Personals

Henry Morgenthau, jr., son of the former United States ambassador to Turkey, has taken office as conservation commissioner of New York. Carl E. Ladd, director of extension at the New York State College of Agriculture, will serve temporarily as deputy commissioner during his sabbatical leave.

Lewis E. Staley is to serve as secretary of the Pennsylvania Department of Forests and Waters under Governor Gifford Pinchot. Before going to South Carolina, where he has served as State forester for the past two and one-half years, Mr. Staley was active in State forestry work in Pennsylvania for 21 years. He will be succeeded in South Carolina by H. A. Smith, who went from a position as district forester in Pennsylvania to that of assistant State forester of Florida.

Seth E. Gordon, for several years conservation director for the Izaak Walton League of America, has been elected president of the American Game Protective Association, succeeding the late Carlos Avery. Mr. Gordon was previously executive secretary of the Pennsylvania Board of Game Commissioners.

John W. Stephen, head of the department of silviculture, New York State College of Forestry, died January 2, 1930. Trained in forestry at the University of Michigan, Professor Stephen joined the faculty of the New York State College of Forestry at the time when it was first organized, in 1912. He was placed in charge of its department of silviculture in 1915, and served in that capacity continuously until the time of his death. Among many books and articles written by Professor Stephen were "Making Best Use of Idle Lands in New York," "Basket Willow Culture in New York," "Forest Conditions in Oneida County," and "Top-Lopping of Branches in Lumbering Conifers."

Alfred K. Chittenden, since 1914 director of the forestry department of the Michigan Agricultural College, died November 1, 1930. Professor Chittenden was a member of the first class graduated from the Yale School of Forestry, that of 1902. He served as a forester both in the United States Forest Service and in the Indian Service of the Department of the Interior. In connection with his educational work at the Michigan Agricultural College he enlarged the college nursery from a small beginning to its present capacity of 3,000,000 trees and developed the Dunbar Experiment Station, at Sault Ste. Marie. His writings include, together with many articles for the quarterly bulletin of the Michigan Agricultural Experiment Station, United States Forest Service bulletins entitled "Forest Conditions of Northern New Hampshire" and "The Red Gum," and Michigan State College bulletins entitled "Forest Planting in Michigan," "Improvement of the Farm Woodlot," and "Christmas Tree Plantations."

The Timber Conservation Board, appointed by the President to find out the fundamental factors responsible for present overproduction of lumber, waste of timber resources, and instability of forest industries and make recommendations as to remedies for these conditions, has the following membership: Secretary of Commerce Lamont (chairman); Secretary of Agriculture Hyde; Secretary of the Interior Wilbur; George D. Pratt, president American Forestry Association; John C. Merriam, president Carnegie Institution; John W. Blodgett, chairman of the board of Blodgett Co. (Ltd.); D. C. Everest, former president American Paper and Pulp Association; Carl Raymond Gray, president Union Pacific Railway Co.; Charles Lathrop Pack, president American Tree Association; John H. Kirby, former president National Lumber Manufacturers' Association; W. M. Ritter, president W. M. Ritter Lumber Co.; L. J. Taber, master, National Grange; and Paul G. Redington, president of the Society of American Foresters and director of the United States Biological Survey. The board's advisory committee is as follows: R. Y. Stuart, United States Forest Service (chairman); E. T. Allen, Western Forestry and Conservation Association; Hugh P. Baker, New York State College of Forestry; S. T. Dana, University of Michigan; Fred H. Fairchild, Yale University; Henry S. Graves, Yale University; W. B. Greeley, West Coast Lumbermen's Association; Charles H. Herty, New York City; D. T. Mason, Portland, Oreg.; George N. Ostrander, Glens Falls, N. Y.; Joseph Hyde Pratt, Chapel Hill, N. C.; George W. Sisson, jr., Raequette River Paper Co.; J. W. Watzek, jr., Crossett-Watzek-Gates, Chicago; Wilson Compton, National Lumber Manufacturers' Association; William L. Cooper, Bureau of Foreign and Domestic Commerce; Charles J. Rhoads, Office of Indian Affairs; Laird S. Bell, Fisher, Boyden, Bell & Marshall, Chicago; and J. G. McGowin, W. T. Smith Lumber Co.

S. D. Marckworth is leaving his position as professor of forestry in the Louisiana State University to accept a similar position in the Georgia State College of Agriculture.

F. B. Trenk, for more than six years extension forester for Maryland, has accepted appointment as extension forester for his native State of Wisconsin, succeeding Frederick C. Wilson. Mr. Trenk received the M. S. degree in forestry from the Iowa State College in 1925. The new extension forester for Maryland is Richard Kilbourne, a 1926 graduate of the Yale School of Forestry who has had three and one-half years' experience with the Tennessee division of forestry.

Howard Hopkins has reported at the Washington, D. C., office of the United States Forest Service as forest inspector in the Branch of Forest Management. Mr. Hopkins entered the Forest Service in 1923, the year of his graduation from the Yale School of Forestry. After several years' experience on the White River National Forest, Colo., he was transferred to the Chippewa National Forest, Minn., as forest examiner, and since January, 1928, he has been supervisor of the Chippewa.

William Maughan has resigned as instructor in applied forestry, Yale School of Forestry, to go to Duke University, Durham, N. C., as assistant director of Duke Forest and assistant professor of forestry. While at Yale, where he received the M. F. degree in 1929, Mr. Maughan assisted in reorganizing the Eli Whitney Forest as a demonstration area and became coauthor with Professor Hawley of the bulletin, The Eli Whitney Forest—A Demonstration of Forestry Practice. He is the author also of the Yale bulletin, The Control of the White Pine Weevil on the Eli Whitney Forest. For three years following his graduation with the B. S. degree in forestry from the University of Minnesota he served as instructor in forest engineering in the New York State College of Forestry.

George M. Gowan, supervisor of the Trinity National Forest, Calif., has been transferred to the California Forest Experiment Station as project leader in fire investigative studies. In this work he is assisted by John Curry, formerly deputy State forester of Maryland, and A. A. Brown, formerly assistant supervisor of the Jefferson National Forest, Mont.

Nils Fornander, a forester of Karlstadt, Sweden, is touring the United States in order to familiarize himself with American logging methods. Mr. Fornander is employed by the Uddeholm Co., which has 600,000 acres of timberland in the Province of Varmland under sustained-yield management, the annual cut averaging about 210,000,000 board feet.

C. M. Granger, director of the survey of forest resources and requirements which the United States Forest Service has under way, is now stationed in Washington, D. C.

Nelson C. Brown, professor of wood utilization in the New York State College of Forestry, has gone on leave for a year to accept a temporary position with the United States Tariff Commission. He will make a study of lumber production costs in the Douglas fir region of the Northwest and in the southern pine region.

J. Bernhard Melin, assistant meteorologist of the United States Weather Bureau formerly stationed at San Jose, Calif., has been made fire weather specialist for the State of Washington, succeeding the late George W. Alexander.

Richard P. Imes, at one time supervisor of the Harney National Forest, S. Dak., has been appointed register of the land office at Billings, Mont.

Felipe M. Salvoza, a member of the 1928 class of the New York State College of Forestry who has received the master's and doctor's degrees from Harvard University, has been appointed instructor and lecturer in dendrology and botany in the Forest School, University of the Philippines.

Thomas E. Carpenter, for the past three years employed as landscape architect and forester at Letchworth Park, near Castile, N. Y., has been appointed as landscape architect in the National Park Service with headquarters at San Francisco.

Ben W. Rowland, formerly employed as a research chemist by the Goodyear Tire & Rubber Co., is now research associate and associate professor of colloidal chemistry in the Institute of Paper Chemistry, Lawrence College, Appleton, Wis. His appointment resulted from the establishment of a research fellowship by the Stein-Hall organization.

Ernest P. Leavitt, assistant superintendent of Yosemite National Park, has been appointed superintendent of Hawaii National Park. Superintendent Thomas J. Allen has been transferred from Hawaii to Zion National Park.

F. I. Righter, who has been acting professor of forest management at Cornell University during the absence of C. H. Guise, is soon to assume the duties of a geneticist at the Eddy Tree Breeding Station, Placerville, Calif.

W. L. Neubrech, a 1927 graduate of the New York State College of Forestry, has resigned as assistant in forestry, Purdue University, to become assistant business specialist with the lumber division, United States Department of Commerce. He is succeeded by Roy Brundage, a fellow alumnus of the Syracuse college.

C. G. Strickland, California forest inspector in charge of the Mount Shasta district, has been made deputy State forester, with headquarters in Sacramento. His successor is E. P. Biggs, formerly inspector in charge of the middle Sierra district, of which Earl T. Barron will now have charge in addition to his duties as inspector of fire control throughout the State. Cecil Metcalf, formerly State forest ranger in Tulare County, has been made inspector in charge of fire prevention and suppression in the San Joaquin district.

Elwin E. Harris has joined the derived products section of the Forest Products Laboratory, to engage in an investigation of lignin. Doctor Harris, who received both the master's and the doctor's degree from the University of Minnesota, has served for the past seven years as professor of organic chemistry in the University of North Dakota.

Gilbert H. Wiggin has been appointed forester in charge of the North Dakota State Forest Nursery, at Bottineau. Mr. Wiggin is a forestry graduate of the University of Minnesota and has had experience in forest research at the State forest experiment station at Cloquet, Minn. He succeeds Sidney S. Burton, now forester in charge of the Southern Great Plains shelterbelt project of the Federal agricultural field station at Woodward, Okla.

Fay G. Clark, for the past 10 years a member of the forestry faculty of the University of Montana, has left that post for a year to study and teach at the Iowa Agricultural College.

Floyd Otter, junior forester on the Lolo National Forest, Mont., has resigned to accept a position at the University of Idaho Forest School, where he will teach silviculture and work for a master's degree.

W. F. Sellers, of the Federal gypsy-moth laboratory at Melrose Highlands, Mass., sailed in October for Europe. He will be stationed at the temporary field laboratory at Budapest, Hungary, and will be associated with P. B. Dowden in the study and the introduction into the New England States of European parasites of the gypsy, brown-tail, and satin moths.

Charles Geltz, recently an instructor in the Pennsylvania State Forest School, is now teaching forestry in Purdue University.

C. N. Mease has been transferred from the post of chief forest warden and district game warden in district 1, North Carolina, and placed in charge of all western North Carolina game refuges.

Joseph B. Pike, jr., a recent graduate of the Yale School of Forestry, is now district forester of the Piedmont section, Virginia.

Bibliography

Timber Growing and Logging and Turpentining Practices in the Southern Pine Region

By C. F. EVANS, United States Forest Service

The latest contribution to the series of Forest Service bulletins on timber growing and logging practice in the various forest regions of the United States is a 111-page bulletin [2] by R. D. Forbes entitled "Timber Growing and Logging and Turpentining Practices in the Southern Pine Region." The purpose of this publication, as stated in its introduction, is "to bring together the gist of what has thus far been learned about the growing of timber" in the South for the benefit of southern timberland owners and others who may be interested in the subject. The guarded claims made in the introduction as to the applicability of the measures advocated in the bulletin are disarming to the critic. Indeed, the presentation seems overmodest in that it commends the publication to landowners only "as a starting point." I believe that it will be accepted rightly as much more than that.

The scope of this bulletin imposed an extremely difficult task upon the author. The southern pine region from Maryland to Texas is by no means homogeneous. Methods that are quite suitable in one part of this territory may not be applicable in another part. This inherent difficulty and the lack of definite information concerning certain elements of the timber-growing

business are met in many instances in the text by giving a range of figures or a choice of methods, the idea being that any local application will fall somewhere within the range. The author recognizes frankly that this will not satisfy the landowner who wants detailed advice adapted to the "individual needs of particular holdings." The point deserves further emphasis.

As in other publications of the same series, the recommended measures are divided into two groups, on the basis of intensity of management—"minimum" measures, which "represent broadly the lowest cost that must be incurred to keep forest land reasonably productive," and "desirable forestry practice," which of course costs more. It seems unfortunate that this distinction had to be made. If the arrangement of material in the text appears clumsy and confusing to the reader, the blame can be placed on this conception.

A brief but, in general, adequate description is given of the habits of growth of the four main species of southern pine—longleaf, slash, shortleaf, and loblolly. It is to be regretted that one of the most important problems concerning longleaf pine, the question as to whether under certain conditions fire is useful in obtaining reproduction, is dismissed with a single unsatisfying sentence. If controlled burning of rough areas prior to seed fall helps to establish longleaf reproduction, as is stated by one of the authorities cited in the list of references, the sooner we know it the better. Perhaps the author had not reached a definite conclusion on this subject.

The 26 pages given to fire protection contain many valuable suggestions. The author's general conception of this job is sound, although obviously some details of his recommendations can not be applied uniformly

[2] U. S. Department of Agriculture Technical Bulletin No. 204. Copies may be obtained free of charge, as long as the supply lasts, from the Office of Information, U. S. Department of Agriculture, Washington, D. C.

throughout the region. Here again the landowner may need to seek expert advice adapted to the particular needs of his locality and holdings. Not many owners will undertake the expense involved in the slash-disposal measures advocated or in the intensive system of firebreaks indicated for slash-covered areas. It would seem that in most cases the same amount of money would buy more protection if invested in detection, patrol, and suppression. I doubt that firebreaks will be needed as a rule for isolated farm woodlands, particularly for 40-acre tracts. Where such tracts are surrounded by cultivated land, very little cash outlay will be needed for their protection. In many cases they will be safe if the owner merely refrains from firing them himself.

In respect to the matter of raking trees in turpentine orchards the bulletin is somewhat behind the present proved practice. Members of State forestry departments and landowners within intensively protected areas in the Southeast will not agree that raking is either necessary or desirable. The elimination of raking has proved to be a most effective fire-prevention measure, and as a result owners of protected lands in Georgia and Florida are drawing their turpentine leases so as to prohibit raking. The rapid development of this practice has come, of course, only within the last year or two, and it is still true that raking is the general custom. The Florida Forest Service has convincing figures to prove that organized protection plus an adequate system of firebreaks is less expensive and more effective than raking.

The part of the bulletin that deals with seed trees, methods of bringing about natural regeneration, and the desirability of obtaining fully stocked stands impresses me most favorably. Here the author has brought together some information that will be extremely valuable. It may in time develop that too much reliance has been placed on seed trees in the reproduction of longleaf pine and that, after all, planting is the cheapest way (the author recognizes this possibility); but for the present the author's views on this subject seem well balanced.

The turpentining practices recommended will no doubt prove very helpful. It is not clear whether the author has in mind naval stores or wood products as the primary crop. At present the landowners in the eastern part of the longleaf and slash pine region undoubtedly are thinking of naval stores as the primary crop. Detailed management plans can not be made until the objective is defined. This applies with special force to thinning methods. In this connection the expressed doubt as to the importance of thinning slash pine stands (p. 93) is surprising. Owners of protected slash pine stands in the Southeast are struggling with the problem of how to thin for best results and with the least expense. They and their technical advisers are convinced that thinnings are necessary. It is estimated that more than 10,000 acres of young slash pine

was thinned in south Georgia in 1930. On many protected areas in this region a few years' protection from fire has resulted in an oversupply of slash pine reproduction, and there appears to be ample proof that partial stagnation follows if such stands are not thinned. The "wrecked" stands illustrated on pages 59 and 60, if protected for 10 years, will require thinning.

Many landowners and foresters will not share the author's gloomy view of the future of much of the second-growth land in the South. Undoubtedly it has been badly treated and the devastated portion (10,000,000 acres) will not recover without artificial reforestation. But experience in slash pine stands does not support the inference (p. 100) that planting will be needed on lands without advance reproduction if all trees suitable for seed production have already been turpentined—which, the author observes, is an almost universal condition in the second-growth stands of the eastern naval stores territory.

A few minor errors in expression are noted. Firebreaks are called "fire lines." "Middle buster" appears as "middle burster." In the introduction (p. 2, line 27) the word "reforestation" is used in a provincial sense to cover all phases of forest practice. In line 7, paragraph 2, page 50, shortleaf pine is referred to as longleaf pine.

It would be impossible in a short review to indicate the full scope of this publication. The bulletin contains a wealth of information and valuable suggestions. It is an outstanding contribution, too ambitious in its conception but offering full proof of the assertion in the introduction that "we know enough now about growing timber in the southern pineries to go right ahead."

A Census of Forest Investigations in the Northeast

A Census of Forest Investigations Under Way in New England and New York, recently compiled by the Northeastern Forest Experiment Station, lists 292 investigative projects. According to investigative field the following distribution is shown: Forest management, 82; forest protection, 56; forestation, 51; forest mensuration, 41; forest ecology, 28; forest utilization, 21; forest economics, 5. Classified according to the agency responsible, projects listed fall into groups as follows: Forest schools, 107; private companies, 52; agricultural colleges and experiment stations, 28; other colleges and universities, 24; the United States Forest Service, 25; other Federal bureaus, 12; State forestry organizations, 21; botanic gardens and other scientific institutions, 11. Descriptions of the 292 projects form a 125-page mimeographed book. So long as the supply lasts, requests for this publication will be filled without charge by the Director, Northeastern Forest Experiment Station, Amherst, Mass.

R'ecent Bulletins on Selective Logging

By A. B. RECKNAGEL, Cornell University

Among the many recent publications on selective logging, the work of Raphael Zon and R. D. Garver and of W. W. Ashe is outstanding. Ashe undoubtedly was the first American forester to write on the subject (cf. his article, "Small Timber and Logging Costs from Profit Standpoint," in the Lumber Trade Journal, November 1, 1914); Zon and Garver were the first to make a full-length study of this important problem. An advance report on the study by Zon and Garver was published in 1927 by the Northern Hemlock and Hardwood Manufacturers' Association of Oshkosh, Wis., under the title "Selective Logging in the Northern Hardwoods of the Lake States." The final report appeared in 1930 as Technical Bulletin 164 of the United States Department of Agriculture.

Zon's and Garver's outstanding conclusions are as follows: (1) Logging costs decrease with increase in the size of the log; (2) overrun is larger in small than in large logs; (3) milling costs decrease with increase in the size of the log; (4) lumber in large logs is of higher grades; (5) a tree must be at least 12 inches in diameter at breast height if the lumber from it is to be worth more than the cost of production; (6) the greatest profit per acre occurs when only trees 12 inches or larger in diameter at breast height are cut.

An important difference between the advance report and the final bulletin is that in the latter the discussion of relative logging costs and values is based upon tree diameters, not log diameters.

Ashe's most recent bulletin on the subject of selective logging is entitled "Profit or Loss in Cutting Shortleaf and Loblolly Pines in Alabama." [3] His analysis regards the tree as the unit. As he says, "while it is customary for the operator to think in terms of logs, so long as this is done it is not possible to reach any conclusion as to what tree it is profitable to cut."

Ashe's findings "show, roughly, that for a band saw-mill operation it costs, including stumpage, twice as much to produce lumber from trees 9 inches in diameter as from trees 25 inches in diameter; that for a circular sawmill operation it costs 65 per cent more to produce lumber from 9-inch trees than from 25-inch trees." They show further that for average-aged second-growth stands the lumber which is sawed from 25-inch trees has an f. o. b. value nearly twice that of lumber sawed from 9-inch trees.

A significant feature of Ashe's logging and mill-cost bulletin is the figures showing the returns per 1,000 feet of lumber that can be realized by cutting to different diameters. These figures show that the maximum returns per 1,000 feet are obtained by leaving all trees under 18 inches in diameter at breast height. In the operations covered by Ashe's study the maximum return per 1,000 feet was $7.67. Such a return makes selection cuttings at frequent intervals profitable in spite of the high cost of railroad construction and band-mill operation. The adoption of such a diameter limit, therefore, tends to prevent abandonment or neglect of cut-over land by private owners.

While selective logging alone does not constitute good silviculture, as these authors point out, it is an important component; it brings in the greatest returns in proportion to volume removed, allows of an early second cut, saves the small trees, and largely solves the small-log problem.

Other papers of recent date which should be noted at this time as evidence of widespread interest in the subject of selective logging are:

1. Selective Logging and its Application in the Douglas Fir Region, by D. T. Mason, in the Timberman, October, 1929.
2. Small Trees Wasteful to Cut for Saw Timber, by W. W. Ashe, United States Department of Agriculture Leaflet 55, January, 1930.
3. The Effect of Tree Sizes on Western Yellow Pine Lumber Values and Production Costs, by W. H. Gibbons, H. M. Johnson, and H. R. Spelman, in the Timberman, 1929–30.
4. The Tree That Does Not Yield a Profit, by W. W. Ashe, in the Scientific Monthly, October, 1930.
5. Selective Logging versus Clear Cutting in Shortleaf Pine, by R. D. Garver, in the Southern Lumberman, October 15, 1930.

Forestation with Poplars in France

Reporting on a visit to France in the summer of 1930 A. B. Stout writes in the December Journal of the New York Botanical Garden on the use of poplar for forest planting in that country. Doctor Stout's observations were made in the region about Noyon to the northwest of Paris and over a considerable area along the Ourcq and Marne Rivers to the northeast of Paris. "At the present time," he states, "the forestry efforts with poplars are more extensively developed in France than in any other country. * * * The principal poplars grown in France for their timber are evidently of three types, known as "régénéré," "angulata," and "peuplier à écorce noire" (also called "peuplier de Caroline"). * * * In making forestation plantings in France, the rule is to use 3-year-old trees that have been grown from cuttings in nursery culture. The trees are frequently 9 feet tall when planted and they make very little growth the first year after the transplanting. It is said that younger trees or cuttings do not succeed. * * * From estimates of yield supplied to the author, it appears that a tree crop is frequently harvested at the age of about 25 years, at which time a yield of 40 or even 50 cords per acre may be obtained. * * * The poplars in France appear to be remarkably free from fungous diseases and insect pests."

[3] Bulletin No. 2, Alabama Commission of Forestry. Pp. 64. Montgomery, Ala., 1928.

Index Published for Society of American Foresters Organs

Completion by a committee of the Appalachian section, Society of American Foresters, of a heavy task undertaken by the section three years ago has resulted in publication of a cumulative index for the Proceedings of the Society of American Foresters, volumes 1–11 (May, 1905–October, 1916); the Forestry Quarterly, volumes 1–14 (October, 1902–December, 1916); and the Journal of Forestry, volumes 15–27 (January, 1917–December, 1929). The committee that prepared the index consisted of Clarence F. Korstian (chairman), Jesse H. Buell, and Verne Rhoades. Copies of this printed index of 111 pages are being distributed at a charge of $1 each by the Society of American Foresters, Hill Building, Seventeenth and I Streets NW., Washington, D. C.

Douglas Fir Yields

By Francis X. Schumacher, United States Forest Service

What is undoubtedly the most complete analysis of the growth of fully stocked stands that has been made for a single timber species in the United States has recently been published by the Forest Service as a bulletin[4] entitled "The Yield of Douglas Fir in the Pacific Northwest," by R. E. McArdle and Walter Meyer.

The yield tables are based upon measurements of 2,049 sample plots having an aggregate area of 1,371 acres; the volume tables were prepared from values of more than 1,900 trees. Most yield tables heretofore published in this country have been constructed from less than one-tenth this quantity of data. This in itself will undoubtedly establish in the minds of foresters and timbermen a great degree of confidence in the work. But the authors have gone further. Supplementary surveys were made to test the relationship of actual to normal stands. These included the running of 62 miles of very detailed strip surveys. The outcome of this part of the work, surprising to one unfamiliar with the region, was the disclosure that over extensive areas actual stand values are approximately 80 per cent of the normal yield table values.

Douglas fir seems to be more variable in its stand characteristics than any other timber species in this country. The University of California has published, within the last few months, yield tables for Douglas fir in that State. Although the growth of the California stands is significantly different from that of the stands in Oregon and Washington, it is interesting to note, these two studies have shown about the same variation of individual stands from normal subregional values for age and site. Following is the comparison of the vari-

ations, expressed in percentage of the standard error of estimate:

	California	Oregon-Washington
Basal area	16.4	14.3
Number of trees	27.0	24.6
Cubic volume	16.3	16.3
Volume in board measure	20.4	20.8

A New Fire Control Bulletin

By Howard R. Flint, United States Forest Service

"The Determination of Hour Control for Adequate Fire Protection in the Major Cover Types of the California Pine Region" is the title of a United States Forest Service bulletin[5] by S. B. Show, regional forester at San Francisco, and E. I. Kotok, director of the California Forest Experiment Station. The bulletin is worthy of study by publicly employed foresters engaged in the administration and financing of large fire-control organizations. The authors attempt, by statistical methods, to establish for each cover type considered the speed of action necessary to limit the area burned over by fires in one year to a maximum agreed upon as permissible for the type. Through the determination of this speed factor it is hoped to bring about an equitable distribution of fire-control funds according to cover type.

Many experienced foresters will question the essential character and importance of the thesis of this paper, set forth in the introductory statement as follows: "Successful fire protection on the national forests or elsewhere requires the solution of four major questions. These are: (1) A determination and statement of a specific objective; (2) determination of the speed or hour control necessary in attacking fires in order to hold burned acreage to the accepted objective; (3) determination of the size and distribution of man power and of fire-protection improvements required to attain the needed hour control; (4) the methods, technic, and training needed to use most effectively the man power and equipment after its arrival at the fire." Rather oddly, the authors mention on page 6 that they have omitted from calculation two national forests in the California pine region, having a total area of 3,000,000 acres, on which the fire-control objective specified by them has already been consistently and cheaply attained. Success in these cases appears to have been fully achieved without any consideration having been given to at least the first two of the alleged major requirements for its attainment.

The statement on page 2 that for timbered types the fire-control objective, in terms of the maximum pro-

---

[4] U. S. Department of Agriculture Technical Bulletin No. 201. Copies may be obtained free of charge, as long as the supply lasts, from the Office of Information, U. S. Department of Agriculture, Washington, D. C.

[5] U. S. Department of Agriculture Technical Bulletin No. 209. Copies may be obtained free of charge, as long as the supply lasts, from the Office of Information, U. S. Department of Agriculture, Washington, D. C.

portion of area that may permissibly be burned over in a year, "is determined from the length of timber rotations in the region and the loss which can be endured without disrupting sustained-yield management plans," will probably be far from reassuring or satisfactory to many thoughtful foresters and conservationists.

The analyses of data and the discussions are of the high standard one might expect from these two authors. There should be many critical readers of the bulletin among foresters and fire-control men.

A School Leaflet on Tree and Shrub Flowers

By W. A. DAYTON, United States Forest Service

An attractively garbed and phrased booklet [6] published by Cornell University under the title "The Flowers of Woody Plants" depicts the inflorescences of native and naturalized woody plants as interesting, profitable, and esthetically valuable objects of study for children. A rather detailed description is given in popular form of the morphology, phenology, and pollenation of the flowers of about a score of familiar trees and shrubs, by seasons. There are 23 half-tone figures of woody plants in bloom, in addition to 4 full-page photographs (including that on the cover, of dogwood in full blossom); and 130 line drawings (illustrating 129 species), most of which are small and compact but very satisfactory. There is also a brief bibliography and an elaborate table of 32 important trees, shrubs, and woody vines, showing their ecology, morphology of both mature plant and seedling, phenology, wood characteristics, enemies, and uses.

Cover Type and Fire Control

By J. A. MITCHELL, United States Forest Service

Recognizing cover type as "an element of basic importance in fire control," S. B. Show and E. I. Kotok present an analysis of the fire problem from that angle in a bulletin entitled "Cover Type and Fire Control in the National Forests of Northern California." [7] Although the bulletin deals with a specific region, the principles evolved and the methods used in developing the data are of general interest. In the words of the authors, "the study aims to distinguish the occurrence and behavior of fire in the major cover types as a basis for fire control." Wholly empirical, the study reveals distinct differences between the major cover types in regard to characteristics that affect the occurrence and behavior of fires.

[6] Cornell Rural School Leaflet, vol. xxiii, no. 4. Prepared by Eva L. Gordon and Paul Kellogg, supervised by E. Laurence Palmer.

[7] U. S. Department of Agriculture Bulletin No. 1495. Copies may be obtained free of charge, as long as the supply lasts, from the Office of Information, U. S. Department of Agriculture, Washington, D. C.

As the authors point out, the occurrence and behavior of fires depend on the character, quantity, and condition of the fuels present, all of which are largely determined by type and the climatic conditions of which type itself is an expression. Thus cover type furnishes an index of the risk of fires starting, season of occurrence of fires, kind of fire to be expected, probable rate of spread, difficulty of control, cost of suppression, etc.

Although no final mathematical expression of the differences between types in these respects is arrived at, tentative figures are presented which serve to indicate the relative hazard prevailing. Attention is called to the inadequacy of present protective effort in certain important types and to various ways in which the situation can be improved. For example, knowledge of the preponderance of fires in certain types serves as a guide to the better allocation of men and protection improvements, and data on the seasonal distribution of fires by type indicate the proper period of employment of fire guards and smokechasers. Similarly, information as to rate of spread and difficulty of control furnishes a valuable guide in determining the "hour control" and the size of suppression crews needed in each type to keep area burned within standard limits. Records indicating the distribution of man-caused fires by type, also, provide a guide to the proper application of measures designed to prevent fires from starting.

While by no means exhausting the subject of cover type and its relation to fire control, this bulletin is a distinct contribution to forest protection literature and indicates the possibilities of further research along this and similar lines.

Recent Books and Pamphlets

Aughanbaugh, J. E.: Recovery of the chestnut in Pennsylvania. 18 pp. (Pennsylvania Department of Forests and Waters research circular 1.) Harrisburg, Pa., 1930.

Bates, C. G., and Zeasman, O. R.: Soil erosion—A local and national problem. 100 pp., illus., maps, diagrs. (Wisconsin Agricultural Experiment Station research bulletin 99.) Madison, Wis., 1930.

Gray, L. C., and Baker, O. E.: Land utilization and the farm problem. 54 pp. diagrs. (U. S. Department of Agriculture miscellaneous publication no. 97.) Washington, D. C., 1930.

Lappi-Seppälä, M.: Untersuchungen über die entwicklung gleichaltriger mischbestände aus kiefer und birke. 241 pp. pl., diagrs. Helsinki, 1930.

Maryland Department of Forestry: Report for fiscal year 1929. 52 pp. il. Baltimore, Md., 1930.

Meyer, W. H.: Diameter distribution series in even-aged forest stands. 105 pp. diagrs. (Yale School of Forestry bulletin no. 28.) New Haven, Conn., 1930.

New Jersey Department of Conservation and Development: Report for the four years ending June 30, 1927. 82 pp. pl., diagrs. Trenton, N. J., 1928.

New York State Reforestation Commission: Preliminary report, transmitted to the legislature February 6, 1930. 6 pp. Albany, N. Y., 1930.

Raine, W. M., and Barnes, W. C.: Cattle. 340 pp. pl. Doubleday, Doran & Co., Inc., Garden City, N. Y., 1930.

Schmidt, W.: Unsere kenntnis vom forstsaatgut. 256 pp. illus. Verlag "Der Deutsche Forstwirt," Berlin, 1930.

Wisconsin State University, College of Agriculture: Making the most of Ashland County land. 30 pp. maps, diagrs. (Special circular.) Madison, Wis., 1930.

Articles in Periodicals

American Water Works Association Journal, September, 1930: Municipal watersheds in the national forests, by M. H. Wolff, pp. 1228-1235.

Canadian Journal of Research, June, 1930: Studies on lignin and related compounds, by H. Hibbert and others, pp. 357-375.

Forestry Chronicle, September, 1930: The balance between cut and increment in Sweden, Finland, and Norway, by P. Bellander, pp. 13-16.

Forstwissenschaftliches Centralblatt, November 1, 1930: Die holzwirtschaft Europas, by T. Streyffert, pp. 825-836.

Indian Forester, October, 1930: Forest and stream flow, by E. Benskin, pp. 440, 442.

Journal of Forestry, November, 1930: A public forest policy, by H. A. Smith, pp. 913-927. December, 1930: The administration of Indian forests, by J. P. Kinney, pp. 1041-1052; Management plans for all-age forests, by D. M. Matthews, pp. 1057-1069; Wisconsin hardwoods and hemlock, by R. B. Goodman, pp. 1070-1075; A method of constructing growth tables for selectively cut stands of western yellow pine, by W. H. Meyer, pp. 1076-1084; Is silviculture possible in America, by W. Shepard, pp. 1110-1118.

Journal of Land and Public Utility Economics, May, 1930: Land ownership, utilization, and taxation in Bayfield County, Wisconsin, by G. S. Wehrwein, pp. 157-169.

National Geographic Magazine, August, 1930: Working teak in the Burma forests, by A. W. Smith, pp. 239-256.

Pan American Magazine, October, 1930: World's future lumber yard, by W. R. Barbour, pp. 267-274.

Pulp and Paper Magazine of Canada, November 6, 1930: Logging, the best means for improving and growing forests, by A. Koroleff, pp. 525-528, 552.

Science, October 24, 1930: A new technique in tree medication for the control of bark beetles, by F. C. Craighead and R. A. St. George, pp. 433-435.

Tharandter Forstliches Jahrbuch, 1930: Die sächsische staatsforstwirtschaft in den letzten 25 jahren und ihre beziehungen zur volkswirtschaft, by Schieferdecker, pp. 537-574.

United States Department of Agriculture Journal of Agricultural Research, September 1, 1930: Relation between moisture content of the wood and blue stain in loblolly pine, by R. H. Colley and C. T. Rumbold, pp. 389-399. October 1, 1930: Effect of cattle grazing on vegetation of a virgin forest in northwestern Pennsylvania, by H. J. Lutz, pp. 561-570. November 1, 1930: A study of the relation between actual and normal yields of immature Douglas fir forests, by W. H. Meyer, pp. 635-665.

West Coast Lumberman, November, 1930: The application of selective logging in the Douglas fir region, by A. J. F. Brandstrom, pp. 27-28, 51.

Recent Publications of the Forest Service

Department Bulletins: 863-D, Forestry Lessons on Home Woodlands (reprint); 1500-D, Gluing of Wood (reprint).

Technical Bulletin 210-T, Correlation Alinement Charts in Forest Research.

Circular 134-C, Suggestions for the Management of Spruce Stands in the Northeast.

Miscellaneous Circular 47-M, What the National Forests Mean to the Intermountain Region (revision).

Miscellaneous Publication 90-M, Range and Forest Resources of Utah, Their Protection and Use.

Farmers' Bulletins: 1117-F, Forestry and Farm Income (reprint); 1405-F, The Windbreak as a Farm Asset (reprint); 1492-F, Arbor Day (revision).

Leaflets: 56-L, Preventing Cracks in New Wood Floors (reprint); 62-L, Why Some Wood Surfaces Hold Paint Longer Than Others (reprint).

National Forest Areas, June 30, 1930.

Report of the Forester, June 30, 1930.

National Forest Administrative Maps: ¼-inch, Pike, San Isabel, Datil, Challis, Salmon, Idaho, Wyoming, Ochoco, Umatilla, Clearwater, Trinity; ½-inch, Pike, San Isabel, Salmon (western half), Idaho, Challis, Tahoe, Ochoco, Ocala, Alabama; 1-inch, Mount Mitchell Division of Pisgah, Catahoula Division of Kisatchie.

CPSIA information can be obtained
at www.ICGtesting.com
Printed in the USA
LVHW021505261118
598291LV00012B/1282